JOHN T[...]

Cobbled [...]

REAL LIFE LESSONS FROM
A HIGH STREET MAVERICK

Caspian

Caspian Publishing

London

First published in 2003 by Caspian Publishing Ltd.

Millbank Tower
21-24 Millbank
London SW1P 4QP

Tel: 020-7828 0706
Fax: 020-7592 8923
www.realbusiness.co.uk

ISBN 1 901844 47 1

Edited by Stuart Rock
Designed by Jenny Eade and Alison Todd
Illustrations by Simeon Stout
Printed by St Edmundsbury Press

CONTENTS

The Timpson story is a remarkable one. Led by John Timpson, the company has become the UK's market leader in shoe repairs, key cutting and engraving. In 1997 it introduced watch repairs, which has now become the fastest growing part of its business. Sales have gone up and employee turnover has fallen.

In the past three years, *The Sunday Times* has come to know Timpson well.

In 2001, Timpson was fourth in *The Sunday Times* list of best companies to work for (the highest placed retailer, and the highest placed UK owned company). This year it continued its outstanding performance with a sixth place listing. It continues to astonish many that a firm of shoe repairers can keep its staff happier than some of Britain's richest management consultancies and legal firms.

John Timpson has also been a regular contributing expert to The Sunday Times Enterprise Network, providing clear, practical advice to scores of growing businesses.

Reading through these articles, it becomes abundantly clear just how and why Timpson has become such a successful company. As John says, it has taken him 43 years to discover that the secret to running a business is based on trust. He listens to his staff, he understands their concerns and he acts in their best interest. He has proved that a motivated, enthusiastic employee will strike a lasting relationship with his customers.

According to our Best Companies survey, staff still feel closely connected to him. An impressive 90 per cent of workers have faith in his leadership; 85 per cent say that he is full of positive energy, and 79 per cent see him as an inspiration. Perhaps more of our business leaders – be they running large or small organisations – could take a leaf from such an example.

Richard Caseby
Managing Editor
The Sunday Times

Acknowledgements

It was very brave of Stuart and Matthew Rock to ask me to write a column for *Real Business*. I am amazed to discover that that was well over four years ago and some 45 articles later. I still thoroughly enjoy the monthly task of plucking out a piece of business life which gives me the chance to poke fun or have a moan.

Thank you to all my acquaintances both inside and outside the business, who have knowingly or unknowingly provided me with worthwhile material.

I would particularly like to thank my son Edward who often edits my final draft and Barbara who types up my notes and often appears in these articles in a starring role.

I would also like to thank the team at *Real Business* who have put this book together.

Finally, I thank my wife Alex, who has not only allowed me to turn writing into a time-consuming hobby, but undoubtedly is the dominant character whose constructive common sense shines through our family life and spills over to influence our business strongly.

This book is dedicated to my grandchildren
— Bede, Patrick and Niamh —
in the forlorn hope that they will grow up
to find a business world with lower taxes,
less red tape and loads more common sense.

1

Introduction

Its activities are mundane, the stuff of daily chores. Getting a key cut. Fixing a watch chain. Buying a new pair of shoelaces or a replacement cigarette lighter. Its presence in daily life is recognisable but hardly glamorous. Its shops are small and usually not in prime sites.

As a retailer, it goes against the conventional. There's no voicemail at its main office. There's little in the way of electronic point of sale in its shops. Stock control is not a priority.

It's widely regarded as one of the best companies in the country to work for and is making a lot of money. It's growing, its young managing director is hungry. And recently it bought Minit UK, Sketchley and Supa-Snaps from the Swiss bank UBS, instantly adding some 500 outlets to the group and making it one of the most powerful brands on Britain's high streets. (The 200 Mr Minits will be re-branded, while the dry-cleaning and photographic brands will be refreshed.)

Welcome to the world of Timpson, the company behind the man who has featured so regularly in the pages of *Real Business*. John's column has a cult following (it's probably one of the magazine's best-read pages) but it doesn't necessarily convey the phenomenon that the company has become. He's too modest, and we hadn't enquired – until now.

"We are the Mr Fixit of the high street," says chairman John Timpson. "We have come from a business that was looked down upon – it was seen as dirty and undesirable to have a cobbler in a shopping centre. So it would be nice to be seen as a special sort of business – something that has a bit of the old lustre that John Lewis or M&S had."

The arrival of the new outlets means nothing less than a "social and business experiment," says John. He's banking that his idiosyncratic "upside-down management" can be replicated across a huge nationwide chain. And in the days following the acquisition, the change has been dramatic. John told his new store managers that, yes, they were allowed to hire a window-cleaner (the poor people had been cleaning their own windows). He told area managers that they could buy their own postage stamps (rather than order them through a head office and – true, this – get them posted back). "I have never seen people turn around so quickly," he says. "We've liberated 2,000 people."

The refugees will be joining a very healthy group.

Turnover at Timpsons has risen steadily year-on-year from £42.4m in 1998 to £54.5m in 2002. Profits have kept pace, from £2.7m in 1998 to £4.8m in 2002.

But, over the same period of time, the number of Timpson outlets (pre-acquisition) remained pretty static. There were 315 in 1998; 331 last year. In fact, the number of staff actually decreased over the same five-year period. Timpson employed 998 people in 1998; in 2002, headcount was 975.

So, with fewer people on its payroll and with a very modest increase in assets, Timpson has boasted a 29 per cent rise in sales and a 77 per cent rise in profits. Don't bother with management gurus. Don't waste your time studying the words of economics commentators. If Gordon Brown, or you the reader, want to see what an improvement in productivity is really all about and what it can mean for a business, look no further.

A lot, as John and his son James will tell you, is down to the people. "It may be the same number but they are not the same people," says John. "They are better contributors now. You can reduce the staff levels in a shop and increase sales. It is an art, not a science. It is about motivating and training people. The money that we have spent on training equates to us being able to take more money: our average 'man take' per week has gone up."

Don't ignore the importance of the stiletto heel either. While they are in fashion, Timpson will always make hay – because if there is one item of footwear that is more likely than any other to need repairing, it's the stiletto. It's doubtful whether Manolo Blahnik knows as much about the fashion for stilettos as John Timpson. "They won't peak until 2005," he predicts, "which will keep our customers coming in for longer. It also exposes us to millions of young, new customers." But stilettos are a fashion. It's a freak peak in the fashion cycle. In the year 2000 the stiletto started its comeback; John Timpson placed a bet with William Hill that the Timpson business would repair over 500,000 pairs of stiletto heels in the year 2004. The odds of 5 to 1 look extremely generous; he looks bound to win. So, after years of struggling, the shoe repair business is now growing and shoe fashion has delivered the Timpson business with a generous profit bonus.

The task for Timpson now is to build up the rest of the business so as to cushion itself for the eventual fall-off in demand from broken, pointed heels. Ten years ago, about 80 per cent of the turnover accrued from shoe repairs and key cutting. Now those two components account for just over 60 per cent. "The historic decline of repairs has been good for us," says John, "as it made us concentrate on other areas."

Shoe repairs used to be a growth business. Sales rose inexorably; each small town supported several cobblers' shops. It all came to a grinding halt in the sixties when cheap imports, followed by training shoes, cut into the traditional business. With winkle-pickers and stilettos in fashion, the sixties were particularly good. But fashion works in cycles. It takes 20 years to move from pointed toes through big round toes and back to pointed toes again. Toes got rounder and heels got fatter in about 1964. Shoe repairers found heel business falling at the same time cheap shoes were eroding their traditional market. Since then, 90 per cent of the shoe repair business has disappeared; instead of having 25,000 cobblers in the country, there are now only 4,000.

Other activities were needed for survival. They tried all sorts of things from knife sharpening to dry cleaning – but the thing that worked was key cutting.

The fastest-growing contributor today is watch repairs, which now constitutes 12 per cent of sales. Managing director son James Timpson remembers the eureka moment, which happened at 9.30am in Eastbourne. "We had installed a watch repair unit there. When I turned up, there was already a queue of people. Business went from £100 per week to £1,200 per week. Bang. Just like that. At Eastbourne we had got the watch repair formula right."

Then there are umbrellas; Timpson is already one of the UK's biggest retailers. And Zippo lighters are a big seller. "We won't sell anything that isn't engraveable," says John. "And we're probably one of the biggest house sign-makers in the UK," he adds.

Growth is opportunistic. A locksmith trial is taking place in the north-west – "this is certainly one with potential," says James. The concept could easily mature into something resembling the old-fashioned ironmonger, drawing in the DIYers who don't want to go to the bland and not always well-informed warehouses of B&Q and their ilk. Other ideas in the offing include free-standing kiosk units for watch repairs and key-cutting.

And Timpson is on its third stab at mastering jewellery repairs. So far, says John, attempts have failed because "we haven't yet found the right buttons to press. I know that there's a secret there but I have yet to discover it." Now it is on trial in Stevenage, with their eye on a while-you-wait service. "We have to win over the hearts and minds of people to make it work."

The success of Timpson, you see, is completely home-grown. "Nobody has walked straight into the company as an area manager," says area manager Tony Sharp. "Most of the area managers are self-taught and have taken on board John's ideas of business and people management."

"Timpson is a business that has been created by its people," says John. "They produce the ideas, they do the training, they increase the turnover, and they understand the special culture here. Much of that success is based on trust and respect. We prefer to nurture the talent that exists within the business rather than risk making outside appointments."

All of the training is done in-house, with the modest exception of some help with video production. Despite it being the standard-setter in its chosen spheres of business, it doesn't do ISO standards. For all its training efforts, it doesn't do NVQs. For all its commitment to its people, it doesn't do Investors in People. "We are a bit peculiar," acknowledges training manager Peter Harris. "We don't fit in."

"We have had several design companies who have come in to help us but they have all failed miserably," observes design and marketing controller Rod Umpleby. "They didn't understand the business. It's a

£60m business with very few employees with any formal qualifications. We tend not to look externally for people."

A Timpson manager tells of one newcomer who took a long time to fit into the fluid structure: "He had to learn to relax and not do everything by the book. Our home-grown style means that people do not have the block of accepting a new initiative."

One of the latest is the "Your Say" scheme, for which area manager Tony Sharp has been the guinea pig. It's not an appraisal but a chance to have a chat over a cup of coffee in a nearby café, he explains. "It's not a moaning session; they want to know how they are doing. They want my perspective," says Sharp. "John Timpson doesn't like appraisals and all the paperwork." Sharp used to take a notepad in but soon stopped. Now he uses his diary afterwards or makes a quick call if there is something that needs speedy attention.

The Timpson management style is about trusting people. John calls it "upside-down management." And it's there to stay. "I believe in trusting people as, in the end, you are better off," he says. "Why not trust people even if there are one or two who will let you down?"

Of course, not everyone gets to grips with it. Not all believe they can really do what they want. Then there are control freaks and others who block the style. And those who don't like delegating.

The style is: do what you think is right. "As long as they have been trained right, I don't care who an area manager hires, how many days they take off, what they look like," echoes James. "If you give them more responsibility, they do a better job."

So matters such as flexitime are unwritten. "You don't have to ask, just make sure that you are covered," explains Rod Umpleby. Every store manager has £500 for discretionary use for dealing with customers. Some store managers, smiles Umpleby, still find this difficult to believe.

It doesn't just apply to those working in the field; it's relevant to the team at Timpson House as well. "We were beginning a massive refit programme," recalls Umpleby. "Three stores a week forever. John and I discussed the list and the priorities. Then he said, 'oh just do it, you are better at this'. But he wants the discussion first."

Even suppliers get the upside-down treatment. "Suppliers' lunch is the ultimate in upside-down management," says Umpleby. "Suppliers normally take you out to lunch. We treat them, tell them about our financial performance, how much money we are making."

John does tend to go on about this upside-down management. It is not, after all, an easy message to get across. But the repetition is all-important. Timpson people have to believe that John believes in it. Only if they believe that, will they then truly understand that they can do what they want to do.

The company has even largely ignored technology, preferring managers' gut instinct. Cash summaries are still written down. The buying department isn't God. The tills in the shops are old-fashioned. "I remember the pre-computer days," says John. "If you have ordered what you want, you will sell it. If you are sent something from head office based on computer data, you ask 'what have they sent us this for'?"

The one thing that remains with John and son James is the selection of new stores (outside London). "This is the one job that we do not trust other people to do," says John. The pair visits prospective sites to estimate how much money it will make. If the rent is £30,000 per annum and they can take £3,000 per week, it's worth taking on. John: "If you show me a shop I can tell you whether it is worth it."

The partnership between father and son makes for gripping viewing. John is chairman, elder statesmen. "I do communications, shop visits, finance, internal PR and whatever James tells me to do," he says. James, the energetic young managing director, focuses on making the existing business hum.

The two work on new ideas together.

So what is the difference between the two? "James adores key cutting, repairing shoes," says one manager. "He's a trader! The difference is that James is John with more confidence. John nearly failed. James has not had that. James could walk into a roomful of strangers, no problem."

Another manager says he didn't talk to John in his first four years – but not because of aloofness. "Deep down, JT is a shy guy," he says. He also reckons that John and James keep score against each other. "I am sure that they have a little book in which they record who has won which battle. John will pay as much attention to a trivial detail as to a major strategic decision. Everything is important to him," he says.

"You can relate to them as they are family people," says Tony Sharp. "You can phone them and they will listen to you. Their secretary is not diverting calls all the time." When Sharp told people at his former employer that his chairman visits his local branch, they could not believe it.

"They didn't know what their chairman looked like."

Ideas that have worked

Mr Men: Timpson used to have a big recruitment problem. Area managers complained that they couldn't find enough qualified cobblers. It was some time before Timpson realised the solution – to look for characters rather than craftsmen. "The best people are those with a great personality," John observes. But that was a difficult message to get across to the area managers who were still looking for cobblers. Timpson started to use "Mr Men" style cartoons, showing the people they wanted and those that they needed to avoid. "That simple method communicated the character of the ideal employee to our recruiters. The quality of our people has improved ever since.

Introduce a friend: Timpson is happy to pinch ideas from others. The company stole its "Introduce a Friend" scheme from Richer Sounds' Julian Richer. An employee is paid a bonus whenever they successfully introduce a new employee. "It has become our best way of recruitment," John observes.

Weekly bonus scheme: Positive, motivated staff who are keen to make money – the attitude is created by the weekly bonus scheme. The calculation is simple; the weekly target is set by the wage bill. The staff share 15 per cent of all sales above the target, with no limit on the bonuses paid on the Thursday of the following week.

Teaching by pictures: "As soon as we had the idea of writing technical manuals in pictures rather than words, we had the start of a training scheme that really works," says John. "Every operation that takes place in the business is now included in a set of guidelines mostly produced in pictures that everyone can understand."

Skill diplomas: All training has a purpose at Timpson – to improve customer service and help staff in the shops earn a bigger bonus. "Individuals are responsible for their own training," says John, "training managers simply help." Skill diplomas enable staff to earn a bigger share of the weekly bonus but they won't get diplomas just by reading books – they have to be able to do the job by passing a practical test.

Excellence centres: In 1990, Timpson bought its first computer engraving machine. It had been originally designed to do industrial work and cost the company £17,000. It was used to produce house signs. This first centralised service has led to the establishment of an excellence centre to carry out large, difficult and complicated jobs that cannot be tackled in a branch. They have increased sales of key cutting, engraving, shoe and watch repairs by accepting jobs that would have otherwise been refused. "In the process, we have improved the service to our customers," says John.

Shop visits: Before buying Minit, John and James Timpson visited every shop every year. With an average of six shops visited per day, they took about 60 days each to complete their task. Most executives would regard that as an unreasonable drain on their time; the Timpsons see it as an essential way of keeping in touch with the business and to meet the people who serve their customers. They have already visited most of the Minit and Sketchley branches.

Customer care courses: Timpson introduced its first customer care courses in 1996. Since then, the company insists that everyone who serves customers has to go on a one day course. "It sends a clear message through the business," says John. Before going on the course, delegates carry out a survey on the high street, taking note of the service at other well-known high street names. "Letting everyone look at life as a customer has made a big difference," says John.

Refits never stop: Every retailer has to keep their shops up to date. "If you stop trying to make things better, you will get worse," observes John. So Timpson never stops tinkering; every unit can expect a refit every four years.

Daily cash: The financial temperature of Timpson is shown each day on a single piece of paper. It shows the bank balance compared with the same date last year. "When you think about it, that tells you a lot about the business," says John.

Weekly profit forecast: "We don't wait for management accounts to find out how we are doing," says John. "Our weekly profit forecast is a back-of-the-envelope figure that keeps our predictions up to date."

Discussion groups: Timpson doesn't do formal meetings. Management debates are seen as soaking up executive time. "But we do listen to what other people say, particularly the people who work in our shops and talk to our customers," says John. "We regularly gather half a dozen people and talk for a couple of hours about their job and our business. We not only learn how things are going, we also get lots of ideas."

Weekly newsletter: Timpson's weekly newsletter performs a central role in creating the culture. Developed mainly by chance in 1996, it now extends to an average of 30 pages in length – full of facts and figures about the business and comments from people working in the shops.

Area profit bonus: In 1988, Timpson faced a temporary fall in profits. "It was our fault," admits John. "We allowed costs to get out of control and our accountants were keen to start a cost-cutting regime. We tried to economise but with little success until we introduced an area profit bonus. By putting area managers on an incentive based on profit, we had delegated the job of controlling costs. They did it magnificently because it made a difference to their bonus."

Videos: Used for training and communicating business strategy, they are sent directly to employees' homes. After all, there aren't any video players in Timpson shops. "It's not just our employees that watch the video," says John, "their families watch as well."

Area teams: John is adamant that a quality service cannot be provided unless shop staff have the necessary support. Area managers are helped by at least three area development managers and a lot of their time is spent training. "By having a team of four people, the area manager has time to think, deal with problems and look after his people. We have found it's best to increase profits by building up the business rather than cutting out costs."

Weekly ring rounds: The Timpson trading week ends on a Thursday, so Friday is the ring round day. All the shops ring their area managers and the area managers ring Timpson. It is a chance for everyone to talk about how well or badly they have done but it also ensures that branch managers talk to their area managers. "It's a great way to communicate," says John.

Branch review meetings: Twice a year, James plus the regional managers, area managers and an area development manager discuss every branch in each area in detail. They talk about everybody who works with Timpson. "It's a good discipline that ensures we don't ignore any of our problems," says John. "It's one of the reasons why we have only four loss-making shops – and those four have to be in profit before the next meeting takes place."

Management

The habitually gloomy finance director. The never-ending search for the illusory person who is really going to transform your business. The tedious hours of business travel. Making the opening speech at sales conferences. Trying to stop people spending money unnecessarily. Many of John's columns have described, quirkily and vividly, the details (and the frustrations) of actually running the business.

2

Me and my FD

Do you remember where you were during the eclipse? I do – meeting the editor of *Real Business* for the first time. It was a tricky encounter.

After watching the eclipse, reflected in the windows of Millbank Tower, we went inside to discuss business. Matthew Rock soon discovered my strong views on accountants and asked me to write about them.

That put me on the spot. How could I write truthfully about accountancy without destroying my relationship with Martin, our finance director?

When I was 17, my father (who regretted not having accountancy qualifications) felt I should leave school to spend a year learning to read a balance sheet. I joined an accountancy firm in Manchester for "work experience."

I couldn't take it. Have you been to Miles Platting? It's a mile north of the city centre and the scene of my first audit. I sat in a cold and dusty mill ticking off figures – £1/19/6d... £1/19/6d... £13/7/2d... £103/1/4d...

After four weeks I conceded defeat, walked to my father's office in Strangeways (just by the prison) and asked for a better job. I got one, as a shoe shop assistant. Even after a degree in Industrial Economics, I never got to grips with a balance sheet.

But I won't make cheap jokes. You see, Martin and I view things from a different perspective. I am a born optimist and he has trained as an accountant. As an economics graduate, I look to the future; Martin looks carefully at the past.

The differences are demonstrated at our monthly board meetings, when Martin reports on our management accounts. It is my regular dose of doom.

Following a good month in August, I looked forward to our September meeting. I thought the unexpected increase in profits and our soaring watch repair sales were good omens. Martin pointed to the poor performance of key-cutting, which (despite an increase on last year) had fallen as a percentage of our overall sales – he saw this as a "worrying trend."

September trade was not so good. At our October board I claimed our disappointing sales were only a temporary blip – "unseasonal weather – good figures last year – seven shops closed for a refit." Nothing to worry about. Martin's long report gave a different spin. "If this month's decline continues for 18 months, we will be trading at a loss."

Martin produces his monthly catalogue of caution until we approach our financial year-end. Then we almost have a communications black-out.

Attempts to obtain a firm forecast of our year-end profits are met with a straight bat. "I wouldn't like to say... It all depends on sales meeting your forecast... There may be some overspends on rent..."

Usually our auditor finds we have exceeded Martin's estimate. A combination of prudent provisions and cautious contingencies allow my monthly prophet of doom to become the bearer of good tidings. But it doesn't always work out that way. Once in a blue moon, profits fail to beat your financial director's careful forecast. That's when you have a real problem. Before long, profits will fall below everyone's expectations and panic sets in.

Inside every accountant is a budding entrepreneur who, on seeing a drop in profit, feels it is time to take centre stage. That is when you must remember the difference between accountancy and economics or, in other words, between hindsight and vision.

Don't let your finance department dictate how to run the business (cost-cutting isn't always the answer). But when it comes to budgets, leave it to them.

Budgets have little to do with running a business, but are excellent for controlling expenses. Budgets also provide a sound basis of communication with your bank manager (another job you should delegate).

Although your bank may be satisfied with budgets and management accounts, don't be deceived yourself. Accounts are riddled with so many estimates, provisions and contingencies, they cannot be trusted. Martin's prudence protects me from the truth – but I have a way to reveal the facts.

Every day I compare our bank balance with the same day last year. Cash in the bank is pure fact – untampered by the art of accountancy. This daily balance is my business barometer.

I showed Martin a draft of this article. "Despite what I have written," I told him, "please don't change the way you are. Be critical every month, keep our bank manager supplied with budgets, keep me guessing at the year-end and, most of all, look after the cash as well as you have done for the last ten years."

Martin was very good about it. He disagreed with some of my comments, but he was happy for them to be published as long as he could write his own piece about how to deal with a chief executive.

3

My big handicap

I usually avoid corporate golf days – five-hour rounds are not for me – but last year I accepted three attractive invitations to play on some of the best courses in the north-west. Each time I played with a bank manager.

Geoff from Barclays has been retired two years, but now claims to be busier than ever. He fits in work for the Prince's Business Trust around two non-executive directorships for ex-clients. During our conversation, we discovered we went to the same school – but he was four years my junior.

Peter, a fresh-faced young man from NatWest, turned out to be 47 years old and on a pre-retirement course. We had a fascinating discussion about how he coped with the problems of negative equity in the late eighties. "I learnt more in those four years than the rest of my career put together," he said. I joked that our game of golf was a good part of his retirement training. He didn't appear amused – he only took up the game two years ago anticipating a further round of NatWest downsizing and early retirements.

Roger, from Lloyds, had a terrible round. His thoughts were elsewhere. "It's make-my-mind-up time. Do I become a bank grandee in London providing senior advice to dot-com protegees, or take the golden goodbye and invest my time in golf or sailing?" I quietly thought that if his sailing is as bad as his golf, he ought to stay in the bank and give much-needed advice to the new economy.

But despite my grey hair, I still felt young enough last Wednesday morning to leave home at 5.30am and beat the M6 Birmingham barrier to reach our Bracknell shop by 9am.

"Are you alone?" said the young manager, surprised that at my age I could still drive and navigate without the help of an area manager. He was so young I asked his age. "Nineteen," he replied. I also found out that his two assistants were 17 and 18 – a combined age of 54. It made me think: the three of them together had lived three years less than I had. No wonder they thought of me as being Grandpa!

But I do have some uses. My eldest children, despite reaching the age where they feel they must offer me advice based on their superior knowledge, still ask for financial guidance and support. Such was the case the other day when one of my younger sons was stranded in London, having been jilted by a hole in the wall.

I rang his bank manager. "He is overdrawn by £34.52. I have written to him three times and he hasn't been in touch, so we are closing the account."

"Have you any children of your own?"

I asked. "No, not yet," he replied. "Well perhaps you don't know that at 19 they are unreliable but by 28 they can become your best customers." "I'm only 28 myself," came the reply.

He offered my son a student account with an immediate £1,000 overdraft.

Last week, I was invited by a friend to substitute for one of the regular golfers in his Tuesday morning four. The heavens opened after nine holes and we scuttled back to the Club House. Eyebrows were raised when I ordered a pint of sparkling mineral water with ice. "On the wagon?" they asked, "No, I am working this afternoon." "Oh, I thought you were retired. Do you still keep a connection with the family firm?" "Yes," I grunted with bad grace. "I run it."

Under my retirement plan – one extra week's holiday each year – this year I am away nine weeks. So you won't be surprised to hear that I write a lot on holiday. My wife Alex peers at me menacingly over her Mills & Boon. "That's not work is it?" she asks. "No," I reply sheepishly. "Just writing another page for that nice editor at *Real Business.*"

In truth, last time I was trying to complete ten tips for our young managers – experience the old man has gained by making mistakes. For a flavour, here are my top three:

1. Don't be depressed by your financial director's board report. His cautious approach is designed to stop your next spending spree.
2. You rarely find Mr Perfect who is waiting to transform your business. Whenever possible, promote from within.
3. Never say: "We are bound to do better next year." You often don't.

On my return from holiday I was keen to run through the full list with my son James. What better venue for the discussion than Delamere Forest Golf Club? We arranged to play 18 holes on Tuesday afternoon. But I never got the chance to pass on my advice to James. The blackboard by the locker room had a notice scribbled on it: "First Tee reserved 2-3.30 for Barclays Bank Golfing Society."

4

Travelling circus

On my desk a collection of tasteless mementoes give astute business advice. "Save Time – Do it Now" is engraved on my clock. "Watch the Cash" says the paperknife. And "Look after your People – They Run Your Business" is printed on a memo pad. My favourite is on the paperweight: "You Won't Find Ideas Sitting Behind This Desk."

The paperweight was bought last summer in America. We needed inspiration to help develop our engraving business. James, my son who avidly follows tips found in business books, felt we needed to clear our minds and get a breath of fresh air by visiting the global village. We spotted a likely source of inspiration on the web: the Things

Remembered chain of 900 engraving gift shops with its headquarters in Cleveland, Ohio.

"It's all right for you going off on a jolly," said Alex two nights before we left. "You realise that you'll miss Henry's parents evening... I suppose you are going club class." I tried to interrupt. "It helps..." "Don't tell me. It helps with jet lag. How many keys will your people have to cut to pay for this little trip?" I tried to hide my excitement, but fact-finding in the States still had its appeal.

All glamour disappeared at Manchester Airport. Holidays were in full swing – we were surrounded by Saga customers and parents with small children. "No problem," said James. "Let's go to the executive lounge." The crowded lounge was full of mobile phones, laptops and briefcases proudly displaying their executive gold card.

Our flight was called. One traveller, wired up to earphones, was so "busy" he continued to speak on the phone until take-off. In the cabin we were surrounded by frequent flyers, none more impressive than the man with a smooth suntan and arrogant moustache who refused the champagne and drank water all the way to Chicago. I calculated the total price paid by my fellow club passengers was £275,000. A lot of good business was needed to pay the fare.

We started to work as soon as we left Chicago airport. James and I tried to clear our minds and find ideas to pay for our trip, but we had to fight the jet lag. With the help of vodka-Red Bull and a serious fillet steak, we lasted until 8pm.

I awoke at 4.30am, watched the news three times and saw highlights of last night's baseball. By 5.30am I thought it was late enough for the gym to be open. I was nearly too late. Thirteen men and women were already cycling in formation. I took the only remaining exercise bike and faced a full-length mirror which showed myself and the other 13 preparing physically for a mentally demanding day at the office.

By 7.30am I was having breakfast surrounded by hundreds of diligent delegates already enormously labelled for a dot-com conference. We queued for breakfast behind T DEAN POOKER, resident vice-president of Tonto Systems, and CHUCK FLITCHETT III, head of communication at Biocom Solutions.

At the next table a group of young people wore grey sweatshirts that announced "wizzcity.com (where it's at)." I guessed that "wizzcity" was at the stage of burning cash. Ten people for bed and breakfast would have cost the company around $3,000.

Our hosts in Cleveland made us feel fantastically welcome. They were filled with boundless enthusiasm and no problems. Anything slightly difficult was called a challenge. They were thrilled to see us. They were thrilled with their level of business – although in the US, this could mean they were only just beating last year. It is difficult to adjust to a world full of optimists.

With my notebook full of ideas, I declared our visit an unqualified success, but the journey home hit trouble. Our flight was delayed by three hours. This gave me plenty of time to observe the American executive and figure out how they justify spending so much time and money on business travel.

While waiting in the bar, four young men were trying to impress two girls at the next table. "What brings you to Ohio?" they were asked. "Been here to close a deal," said one. "And failed… but I got our target to write a note saying I gave a great presentation. It'll soften the blow when my boss gets the $20,000 travel bill."

"How did you get on then?" said Alex, 12 long hours later. "Found any ideas that are going to make our fortune?" "It was just as I expected," I replied. "If we look at the Things Remembered web site, I'll show you." "Just a minute,"said Alex. "I thought you went for new ideas... and yet you found exactly what you expected." I changed the subject quickly. "Oh I forgot. I bought you this." When she opened my present, she smiled. It was a paperweight engraved with this message: "However far you travel the best ideas are at home – ask your wife."

5

Praise indeed

Every three or four weeks Barbara, my secretary, insists that we go through my diary. She fondly believes that this attention to detail saves me from double booking and social disaster. We were comparing diaries two weeks ago when I spotted something odd. "What's this on March 14?" I asked. "I can't remember arranging to go to Denbigh." "Let's have a look," said Barbara. "It's not Denbigh, it's the dentist, you can't even read you own writing. It's the day after you have scribbled AM which, in case you were wondering, is an Area Managers Conference."

I was hardly likely to forget the area managers meeting. Three times a year, we are put on trial. During the conference we do our best to tell them everything about present performance and future prospects and provide a range of tips to help them do their job better. In the evening they pull us to pieces in the bar.

I get the most difficult job. I open the conference. Within an hour of getting off the motorway, the area managers are sat watching me talk through the figures for the last quarter and strategy for the next 12 months. They all watch, but they don't listen. They just want to get back to their mobile phones and follow up the sickness problem in Scunthorpe, the re-fit in Rotherham and a customer complaint in Cumbernauld.

On the second day of the conference I started my session talking about the importance of giving praise.

I passionately believe that middle management should spend more time praising people and less time issuing oral warnings. But the rules are now so heavily in favour of the unscrupulous employee, managers are worried that gratuitous compliments could be used against them in a future tribunal.

In my experience, the words "well done" can be more welcome than a financial bonus. I try and praise a few people every week, usually with a handwritten note, but my handwriting has become a bit of a company joke. "Perhaps we can buy you a laptop for your birthday," said one of the area managers. "Then you can praise people with e-mails and people will actually be able to read what you have to say."

The following day, I rushed to arrive on time at the dentist, and spent the next 35 minutes staring at a sign that read: "Please be patient, computer system just installed." The receptionist woke me up when it was my turn at last. "Any problems?" said the dentist as I sat in the chair. I considered complaining about the wait but thought better of it – this man had a drill in his hands. "No, everything is fine. Just come for my normal check up."

The dentist got to work immediately. "Sorry about the delay," he said. "Hope you won't be late for anything important." I couldn't respond, with a mouth filled by hands and mirrors. "The computer will be great when we overcome the teething problems. Do you want to rinse out?" he asked. "They say that at my office," I said. "You don't have mouthwash at work do you?" said the dentist with a smile. "No, they say that the computer will solve all our problems."

I was too late for our morning meeting, so I called in at our Northwich shop to see why Wayne is doing so well. "Never looked back since the computer engraver arrived," said Wayne. "I am all for this modernisation. I admit we had a few teething troubles, but it will be fantastic when we get it right."

I wandered into the back room to look at his figures and noticed a scrunched up memo in the waste paper basket. Being curious, I unfolded it. It had been produced by his area manager on a new laptop.

MEMORANDUM
To: ALL BRANCHES LISTED BELOW
(Ten branches were listed in alphabetical order).
"Congratulations on an excellent increase in turnover last week, I appreciate all the effort you have put into achieving this performance."

It wasn't surprising Wayne had thrown that memo into the bin; his area manager hadn't even bothered to sign each letter individually. Praise should be personal, not served up in a circular.

"I am glad you didn't throw my letter in the bin," I said to Wayne, spotting a handwritten note I had sent him six months before, pinned up on the wall. "Oh, I'm pleased you saw that," said Wayne. "I've had a bit of difficulty with your handwriting. I am still trying to work out what it says."

6

Why do we bother with budgets?

Things got quite heated at a recent board meeting when we discussed capital expenditure. The personnel manager had submitted a request for the ratification of £1,500 for a PC, printer and the necessary software required for a new member of his department. "Is this within his approved budget?" I asked Martin, our finance director. "No, but it's for ratification." "You mean we have already spent the money?" "Yes, the equipment was delivered last week." "I don't know why we bother with budgets," I said somewhat testily. The directors could see I was

35

unhappy. We had a long discussion about cash control and, as a result, I sent out a note to all senior managers reinforcing the importance of formal board approval for every capital project.

I try hard not to talk business when I get home, but Alex seems to sense when I have something on my mind. That night, thanks to M&S and the microwave, I cooked a typical modern dinner, cod mornay for me, and vegetarian korma for Alex who was watching *Eastenders* while I played with the *Telegraph* crossword. "You look pretty grumpy, what's the problem?" asked Alex. "It's nothing really, just a few things at the office that are getting up my nose. Sometimes I think we are playing politics rather than running a business. You will never guess what happened today." Alex didn't guess because she was too engrossed in finding out who shot Phil.

"Are you going to the office tomorrow?" was her unconnected response. "Yes, it's a busy day, starting with our shoe repair manager at nine o'clock." "That's lucky, you can ask him about my mother's shoes that I gave you to have mended two weeks ago, and by the way, when I borrowed your car the other week, I noticed it has done 90,000 miles. It's about time you changed it." I agreed and returned to the *Telegraph* crossword, "three across, intriguing plot amid ideal husband (eight). "

My memo produced plenty of people wanting to see me about their vital capital expenditure plans. John, the shoe repair manager, stressed the urgency of buying ten new stitching machines. There was a special discount, but it was only available until the end of the month. If John waited for the next board meeting, we would miss the opportunity of a massive saving.

John was followed into my office by George, who heads the computer department (currently the biggest offender when it comes to spending capital). George wasn't interested in buying another computer; on this occasion he needed a car for a new programmer, who would only join us if we could provide something better than the Ford Mondeo currently on offer.

But it wasn't the people who came to see me that got up my nose, it was those who were spending money behind my back. For three weeks I thought that the girl who often parked her car next to mine was one of the auditing team, until I realised she was still there when the auditors had finished their job. I checked with personnel. "She is the new assistant in the training office," they told me. "She started as a temp when Gillian was off and was so useful they decided to take her on permanently. They thought you would approve because you are so keen on training."

Rod, our property manager, overheard the conversation. "That reminds me," he said, "I didn't mention the new lavatory." "What new lavatory?" I asked. "The extra one we now need because of the increase in staffing levels. It's a health and safety requirement."

Martin, my finance director, was clearly worried when he came into my office. "Your memo has brought a lot of capital expenditure items for approval at the next board meeting," he said. "It shows that too many people were spending the money first and asking for approval later. This month, the requests include five new computer key-cutting machines, a laptop for each area manager and a desk for the new girl in the training department. Oh, and by the way," said Martin sheepishly, "can you approve two more PCs for finance?" "When do you need them, Martin?" I asked. "Well, actually they were delivered last Thursday."

I read the riot act at the board meeting. "There's absolutely no point in our giving formal approval when the money has already been committed before the meeting. We have to put a halt to all this nonsense. I am going to impose a complete ban on new expenditure for the next two months." It worked. Everyone seemed to toe the line and instead of spending money, devoted their time to complaining about the lack of resources. Hardly anything was approved at our next board meeting.

I must have looked relaxed as I tackled the crossword that night. "Solved the problems at the office then?" asked Alex. "Yes I think so, we had a good board meeting. Cash-flow looks good, everything is under control." "Sounds like a boring meeting to me," said Alex. "Didn't you spend any money?" "Not much, we just approved the capital for a new car." "I thought you had imposed a total spending block. Whose car was it?" "Mine."

7

In conference

I put junk mail straight in the bin and thought I had taught my son James to do the same. But recently he entered my office bearing a brochure from a retail magazine. "Look at this conference," said James. "If three directors go, two days would become a board retreat. We could forecast the future." I didn't like to say board retreats often lead to disastrous decisions. If directors go away together, it's better to play golf than talk business.

"You realise it's nearly £1,000." (I hoped to appeal to his inherited mean streak.) "But we are up for an award," he replied. "We entered the customer care category and are short listed." I was unimpressed. "We've been short listed before but cobblers never win." James persisted "We'll find out at the dinner." Dinner! That's another £100.

Six weeks later James, Patrick and I collected our badges from registration. About 400 eager executives were already mingling in the room where I was given coffee and a conference pack. They might have provided ideas for an article in *Real Business*, but with conference pack in one hand and coffee in the other, it was impossible to shake hands with other delegates. Instead we sat in the conference hall next to a man already busily making notes in his folder. I looked at his badge, 'John Grubbins AFK Consultants (Maidenhead). ' He was checking the list of delegates looking for likely customers.

I listened intently to the first speaker, conscious I'd paid £100 for each 45 minute session. The second speaker was more difficult to follow, a Japanese who had come to show the nation of shopkeepers how to succeed at retailing. His English was good but not good enough to hold my attention. I looked round the audience. Mine was not the only wandering mind. I saw doodlers, thumb twiddlers, watch watchers and two more consultants ticking off names of possible clients.

At coffee I was about to mention the difficulties of the foreign accent when Patrick said the second speaker was the most impressive he had heard for years. I nodded in agreement. "A clear example," said Patrick, "of someone who keeps things simple and makes them work."

After every session, there were questions. As the microphone went round the room, I wondered whether I should volunteer but I was too nervous. There was no need for my question – the floor was full of consultants sizing the chance to announce their name and where they came from. "John Jefferson, On Line Solutions," or "Paul Sheffield, Test Shop International." I admired the honesty of Fred Hutchins who introduced himself as "solicitor and general hanger on." Lunch was a pasta and fizzy water affair. The dining area was lined with sad-faced exhibitors who had paid lots of money for a stand that everybody ignored.

After lunch, I added to my dotcom phrase book. "The internet is no longer an open ticket for open cheque funding. The difficulties of players like boo.com were pure preplay; we now deal with customers who have lost their on-line virginity; everyone must restructure strategy into the digital age." My notes record I saw the first sleeping delegate at 2.32 pm.

When the last session finished, I went to the bar with James and Patrick. "Have you noticed," I said, "How many consultants, accountants and bankers are here?" "No I haven't," said Patrick, "I was too fascinated with the speakers. It's such a clear message, the successful businesses keep it simple." I agreed. It had been an excellent day.

That evening, The Great Room at the Grosvenor House was full of corporate entertaining. 1,600 people went to the banquet, some hoping to see a repeat of last year's performance when a chief executive was ultimately fired for pinching a girl's bottom. The only excitement I was likely to encounter was the awards ceremony. I worked out how to get from our table to the stage to receive my prize. I needn't have bothered, they didn't give the cup to a cobbler. With nothing to celebrate I went to bed, but most captains of the High Street had a late night.

The next morning delegates found it difficult to stop yawning, but still had pens poised waiting for the critical idea that would pay the conference fee. Minds (numb from the night before) found it difficult to find a gem hidden amongst the jargon. "You must become best in class by attracting the Millennium Generation and comprehend how changing lifestyles create different dynamics in today's spending pattern." Even Patrick started to fidget. Scratching his head, he leant over and whispered "Why can't they talk simple English?"

After lunch we got the American perspective, a look at retail from lots of angles. So many angles he overran. Before he finished the audience started to disappear. They had trains to catch, phone calls to make and businesses to run. I too had heard enough, I put the conference pack in the boot of my car and drove to Hammersmith to meet our new shop manager.

Three weeks later James saw the folder lying in my boot just where I left it. "You didn't think much of the conference did you?" "It was alright," I said blandly, and changed the subject. "There is something I wanted to tell you. I have written a new version of our company strategy. It's called "Keep it simple."

8

Think of a number, any number

In 1980 I was invited to talk to a cobblers' conference in Guernsey. I knew shoe repairing was a declining business and that many operators had their heads in the sand, so I decided to give it to them straight.

I showed a series of graphs charting the decline of the industry. My figures revealed that 65 per cent of the market had disappeared in 15 years. As I went on to forecast future and further decline, delegates became so worried that they didn't notice the words at the bottom of every chart: "Source – Imaginary Research Ltd." I hadn't been able to find any statistics or information about our industry so I just made the figures up.

Three weeks after my talk, I received a call from the *Financial Times*. "I understand you have some facts about the shoe repair industry," said the journalist.

"Sort of. But I made them all up." "That's a pity," he replied. "I have to write about your trade and yours are the only figures I can find."

That's when I discovered that a vivid imagination can be almost as good as market research and comes at a much cheaper price.

Sitting in a doctor's waiting room a few months later, I compiled a shoe industry fact sheet. I wrote it had been discovered that people in Swansea and Glasgow have the smallest feet in Britain while the biggest feet are found in Plymouth. The press release revealing these "facts" was issued on a quiet news day. Camera crews were despatched to Plymouth, Swansea and Glasgow and national papers from *The Sun* to *The Times* gave us the free publicity we were seeking.

We tell every new employee that they must be 100 per cent honest, but there are times when you should tell a lie for a good cause. Business plans are the best example. Banks back figures in preference to flair. They need something to stick in their computer so they can carry out a sensitivity analysis. Everyone knows business plans are the extrapolation of dreams, but as long as your numbers show sales rising faster than costs, there is every chance that the bank will lend you the money.

And being economical with the truth can be a real time-saver, too. When I first launched our company newsletter, I asked each senior manager to make a contribution. Despite several reminders, no-one replied; they were all far too busy. In despair I wrote the articles for them, and showed them the copy the day before publication. No-one objected or made any comment. In the next edition, when I published an interview with our personnel manager, I didn't bother to talk to him at all. I just made it all up. Sitting at my desk I dictated both my questions and his replies. Did he complain that I had put words into his mouth? Not in the slightest. He was flattered to be featured in our first personal profile.

Sadly, our employees don't take any notice of my opinion when they can hear the views of their fellow workers. So I find it useful to communicate any major change with an employee's quote supporting it. Sometimes they are anonymous, "from an experienced long service employee." Others mention someone by name: "One of the best moves the company has ever made," says Darren; "It will certainly increase my sales," enthuses Kath. I ring them up to tell them that they are going to be quoted and everyone seems happy to see their name in print.

These "lies" save time, avoid market research and save you a lot of money. But be warned. If lies are so useful, it stands to reason that other people will be lying to you. Few of us are willing to admit how often we are taken in by clever salesmen. Most of us believe what we read in the newspapers. Every day we receive loads of false information, much of it disguised as official statistics. Even the government is guilty of it; although of course the government doesn't lie, it spins. I invent facts to explain the truth, but the government uses real facts to create a false impression.

It is advisable to know your business inside out before you start inventing stories. As long as your fictitious facts back up the truth, you will create a happy workplace with an open and honest environment. Our annual attitude survey asks how well employees feel they are informed about developments within our business. Over the years we have developed such a reputation for free and frank communication that one employee suggested we should tell everyone the facts behind any rumour before it even starts going round the office.

Our survey results show that open communication, be it true or false, is better than no communication at all. So that proves it: a little bit of spin and a sprinkling of white lies are good for business. But be warned, that might be another home truth produced by "Imaginary Research Ltd."

9

One gnarled CEO... going cheap

One Sunday in September, I was watching Christmas toy adverts on TV with our foster child, when Alex asked an incisive question. "Why don't you advertise? Everyone else does, they don't do it for fun." Our shop managers ask that, too, when business is bad. They expect me to spend a fortune advertising to increase turnover by one per cent. I know different.

Seven years ago I vowed that if our profits reached £2m, I would spend £400,000 on advertising to see what happened. Profits did increase, but I spent the money on training instead. The result was stunning. Our service improved dramatically and lots of customers provided free advertising by recommending us to friends.

I have some bad experiences of advertising. The worst concerned a venture called "Key Call," a new service for motorists to "sign up, register your key details and if you lose your keys, our man on a motorbike will bring a spare set within two hours, whether you are stuck in Stranraer or stranded in Stalybridge."

I was advised that direct marketing would soon build a big customer base. A man called Jed insisted I spent £10,000 on focus groups before investing real money. To Jed, all business could be boiled down to mathematics. Carry out quality research, plug in the facts, flex a few probabilities and your return on investment is guaranteed.

Using pure logic, Jed persuaded me to spend £35,000 on leaflets inserted into national newspapers. This would, he claimed, bring sales of £20,000 in the first year. "That's not a good deal," I said. "The advertising costs more than the sales." Jed could not believe my stupidity. "It's an incredible conversion rate," he said. "Our research proves a fantastic 0.05 response, and you are building a database you can work for years." As it turned out, Jed had his sums wrong. Perhaps he put his decimal point in the wrong place. The £30,000 produced a mailing list of just ten people, including Alex and her cousin from Leatherhead.

Some say that half of all advertising is wasted, but no-one knows which half. I now understand how some advertisers waste money. One Sunday outside our newsagent, shortly after pulling the plug on "Key Call", I saw a man by a litter bin methodically shaking each newspaper until he had removed all the leaflets hidden inside.

Every November we go on holiday – usually a spartan trip to Stornoway. This year Alex deserved some TLC, following a successful hip operation. We went to Mustique. I forgot about business, read five books and had a tennis lesson every afternoon, hoping to acquire a Bjorn Borg top-spin backhand.

As I handed over $500 plus tip to the helpful professional, he said that my game was "much better but you should buy a tennis machine and practise on your own at home." I told Alex, hoping it might get on her Christmas list. "Don't you remember?" she said. "This expensive holiday is our Christmas present, we are giving each other a small stocking."

I returned to a pile of personal mail. Most were envelopes labelled "important" and "urgent." Sky Television wanted me to subscribe for more channels. BT says I am paying too much for my calls, and for another £25 they can save me money. Three identical envelopes to "Mr Simpson" advertised loans at a fantastic rate of interest. The Norwich Union offered special car insurance for people with my postcode; the urgent letter from a stockbroker to Mr William Timpson started "Dear Sir or Madam." My fax machine was as busy as the postman, churning out offers to fly to European cities at cut-price fares.

But my mailbag was modest compared to Alex. Alex is a serious Christmas shopper. Five children, three grandchildren, and a wide circle of friends get the full treatment. She hits Chester and Northwich like a white tornado but still has room to buy mail order. Every year we receive more catalogues. Soon we will have to get a bigger letterbox.

At Christmas, I benefit from Alex's study of the "Innovations" catalogue. Last year I became the proud possessor of a nose hair trimmer, a digital car compass, a computerised skipping rope, an electric blackhead remover and spectacles that help you watch TV while lying flat on your back.

Two days after I sent this column to *Real Business*, a man knocked at our door. "Can you sign?" he asked. He had a big parcel. I signed the delivery note, wondering how much money Alex had spent, then saw the top of the box. "Wrong way up, Tennis Machine." Clever Alex. Her catalogues had produced just what I wanted.

As the man left, the phone rang. It was the editor. "So you don't like leaflets in magazines?" he said testily. "Erm, yes," I replied nervously. "Have you seen *Real Business*?" he asked. "Yes," I said, suddenly realising where he was coming from. "One of the leaflets we put inside our magazine advertised your book *Dear James*. Sales have been excellent recently." As they say, half the money spent on advertising isn't wasted.

It's the next thing on my list...

When I was a 17-year-old shop assistant, I couldn't understand why decisions took so long. It was clear that the brown brogues were over-priced, we were short of black socks and our window displays needed changing. If this was obvious to a 17-year-old, why didn't management do something about it?

Luckily, I had the chairman's ear. I helped him wash the dishes every night. I envied my father's position of power. If ever I became chairman, I would soon sort things out. I naively thought people do what they are told and everyone is interested in getting things done.

It's not that easy. I have just had a frustrating week, which has shown how people get in the way of progress. It started at Monday's management meeting. I don't normally attend, but I dropped in to check progress. The minutes showed evidence of efficiency, with executives' initials in the margin where action was required. George, a lifetime administrator, had his initials all over the minutes. "That remains an ongoing matter," he replied when first asked to report progress. The next time, he said "our internal discussions have not yet come to a conclusion. We hope to make a decision in March."

George had done nothing, but had an answer for everything. "It will be one of the next things I do," he replied to one point, and to another, "in my considered view it would be wise to defer the judgment." He was a complete "spin doctor" of inactivity.

On Tuesday, I was glad to go out visiting some shops, free from meetings and memos. It was a refreshing day spent talking to people who look after customers and don't bother about office politics.

But nothing is perfect. On the journey home, I phoned Richard, the area manager, to run through the faults I found.

"Why are there no umbrellas on display in Basingstoke?" I asked.

"Security," said Richard. "They are very light-fingered in Basingstoke."

"They won't sell in the stock room," I insisted. "And the key machine in Maidenhead needs a new cutter."

"You're right," he replied. "I'm just about to send the order."

But I wasn't finished. "Joanne the apprentice hasn't cut a key yet."

"Health and safety," he said. "I haven't given Joanne a risk assessment, it's on my list."

"Finally," I said, "that tall woman at Winchester has an appalling attendance record, she shouldn't be on our payroll, she hardly ever works for us."

"I am on to that one," said Richard. "But disciplinary procedures always take time."

Back in the office I got my monthly lecture from Barbara. "You want everything done yesterday. Life is not like that. People go at their own pace."

I went to see Dave in display. "None of the shops are using the new pet tag display," I said. "Not my fault," said Dave. "I sent an e-mail to the area managers, I can't go to every shop and do it for them."

Barbara was waiting for me back in the office. "The young people you selected for the fact-finding trip to Chicago are here with their report," she said.

The next half hour restored my faith in human nature. Four enthusiastic young people bubbling with great ideas.

"You look better now," said Barbara when they had gone. "They had loads of good ideas," I said, "but their mailing list suggestion was something I proposed three years ago, and no-one took any notice." "They probably will now," said Barbara. "They are much more likely to follow their ideas than yours."

That night Alex reminded me to tidy the study. Throwing out files takes time, especially if you read them all. I found my university exam papers. I studied economics, but demand curves and Keynes' monetary theory have been of little use in my career.

I eventually found a question I understood, about the "Hawthorn Effect", an experiment in South America in which they increased factory lighting, causing production to go up; then reduced the lighting and production went up further. That's like our shop refits: they make little difference to customers, but have a big impact on our staff. A new layout or different colour scheme gives them an excuse to do better.

"That's the challenge of business," I philosophised, as I left the office on Friday to drive to the golf course. Overcoming people's natural inertia by clever communication. All the excuses disappear as the team attacks in-trays with renewed vigour, and tackles problems head on. The week had ended on a positive note.

"I have been thinking," said my son James on the first tee. "Although Oliver has 33 years service, everyone knows he's a passenger. You said you were going to talk to him."

"I know," I replied. "I have it very much in mind, but employment law is terribly tricky these days. I think it's wise to wait before making a move."

11

Blind data

Every two years I visit the Retail Week conference to keep abreast of modern thinking. This year nothing had changed. The same mixture of middle management posers had their pens poised to impress their boss. A few 'Captains of Industry' gossiped with peers and a battalion of consultants networked for new clients.

"You always learn something here," I overheard during coffee on the second day. What had I learnt? Sadly it taught me I am getting old.

I was surrounded by younger delegates and even the speakers seemed young. To make matters worse, my son James was invited to the VIP lunch while I faced eating a finger buffet trying to avoid consultants looking at my badge to see if I was worth an approach.

Life has moved on since I started work 43 years ago. In 1960, the shop tills were simple adding machines, shop managers ordered their own merchandise and kept stock records in a debit and credit book.

In 1961 I had my first glimpse of the future. We got a computer, an enormous air-conditioned room was filled with grey boxes and disc drives twitching throughout the night. The computer took control of our warehouse, organised the payroll and ran stock control.

For 40 years I have seen a string of ideas designed to help run our business better. Each had promised prodigious profit growth. Most modern managers can't contemplate how we survived without this sophisticated support. But I simply wonder why today's businesses aren't more successful.

A few years ago, we looked at a possible acquisition. I was given a mound of paperwork proudly produced by a new £2m EPOS system. It gave sales breakdowns by day, price, colour and by anything else you could imagine. A team of young graduates enthusiastically analysed the information at head office, apparently unaware the business was losing £3m a year and was fast running out of cash. Companies rely too much on intelligent graduates with complete faith in computer data when it's wiser to employ ordinary folk with lots of charisma and common sense.

Before lunch we were treated to a session on technology. "You may be disappointed to learn," said the first speaker with refreshing honesty, "that for the next hour, you will be addressed by an accountant, a consultant and an IT expert." Five minutes later the first delegates headed for the bar.

The consultant tried to grab our attention. "Just imagine," he said, "life in ten years time. Your fridge orders your food, the internet links to a mobile phone on your wrist giving real time information to debungle the specificity of the market place. To be best in class, you receive fast track solutions to address lifestyle values. In a multi-band global environment, IT is here to release your ability. Help the top line, shave the middle line and grow the bottom line..."

I left him to lecture and disappeared into my imagination. I was visiting Bluewater in 2013. The Bluewater finger print security device announced my arrival to the shopping centre computer, and my wrist phone was bombarded with details of my favourite products. Not just "buy one, get one free", but "buy four, get five more" and "buy 100 and have a half-price holiday".

Within seconds I knew where to buy the cheapest Virgin loo paper, easyGo opera tickets and Man Utd condoms. While I received information about Bluewater, Bluewater heard all about me. They knew my time of arrival, my age, weight, health, and where I go on holiday. My computer said "go to Argos," where I used one of 100 user-friendly consoles to register my requirements. Packages were produced by a jolly robot who took money off my wrist computer and sent detailed data to senior management who operated from Argos head office in Bangalore.

As I left Bluewater, a woman spat on a cash machine that used saliva instead of pin numbers. "Bloody nuisance," she said, "old fashioned shops that insist you pay cash for things like shoe repairs."

My son James was lucky. He missed the technology talk, leaving early to attend a parents' evening. He gave me his invitation to the VIP lunch where I sat next to a Champion of the High Street. He listened with disbelief when I said we don't use EPOS. Our buyers have very few figures but are well informed. To find out what's going on they visit our shops and telephone branch managers. It might be old-fashioned, but it works.

I left feeling older but pleased I hadn't been seduced by consultants with smart solutions designed to help intelligent young people run my business from head office.

That was enough of conferences for another two years. I looked forward to driving home. I switched on the satellite navigation system, rang Alex on the mobile and told her my computer estimated I'd be home in time for dinner.

12

Public speaking

A barrister I met at a drinks party struggled to be heard over the hubbub. "What do you do?" he asked. Resisting the temptation to claim I am a cobbler, I said I run some shops called Timpson. He had never heard of us.

The following day, shocked by our poor public profile, I rang Michael, my spin doctor. "We should be better known," I said. "Publish a book," said Michael. "It's the modern way to build a reputation". 18 months later I published the book with my friends at *Real Business* and for three years have invaded their magazine with my monthly column.

Spin doctor Michael had another idea. "Go on the lecture circuit." He wrote to 20 universities and business schools offering me as a management guru. In six weeks we received two replies. One college pitched to do a marketing project and my old university wrote asking for sponsorship.

I had forgotten about public speaking when, six months later, a department stores group asked me to talk at their annual conference. I compiled a pictorial PowerPoint presentation and arrived for dinner the night before my talk.

Over a drink I met an American speaker. "Have you written a book?" he asked. "Yes," I replied proudly. "I've written five," he said. "All best sellers." It was my first hint of the competitive edge between speakers.

My presentation went down fairly well and during the next fortnight I received two more invitations. A local Rotary Club was keen to hear me. Although the date clashed with a Manchester City match, I turned up for dinner with 20 Rotarians (the chairman said they usually got more for a good speaker). Three left before my talk began.

Breakfast with a Chamber of Commerce in Kent was more successful. They agreed to donate a substantial sum to Childline as my fee – the secretary was so enthusiastic, he promised to organise a sponsored walk to swell the charity's funds. A man of his word, he raised £5000, but sadly for ChildLine, he went missing together with the sponsorship money.

Next came a surprising request. Ken, my dentist, with his fingers in my mouth said, "I understand you do a bit of speaking." By the time he asked me to rinse out, I was booked to talk at his dinner club. "It's my turn to find a speaker," he said. "I was getting pretty desperate."

Some speaking engagements didn't go according to plan - like the Teachers' Convention in Surrey, where there was no projector. And the Department of Work & Pensions woman at an IoD Conference who claimed my slides contravened the concept of equal opportunity.

I trotted out my trials and tribulations to guru Michael. "At least the Timpson name is starting to be noticed," he said.

The next day, I was invited to talk at a high profile convention, involving captains of industry and a cabinet minister. I was flattered. Michael was right, word was getting round. I accepted the invitation without thinking. I sat through the full day, to pick up tips from experienced speakers.

I learned a lot, mainly by watching the audience. They yawned doodled and scratched their nose. They suffered death by PowerPoint. The spoken word was projected on the screen, while delegates flicked their conference pack to count the slides to come before the speaker could sit down.

After lunch, a woman spoke passionately about producing a positive culture in difficult times, and overran by 20 minutes. Succeeding speakers tried to catch up but we were still late for tea.

I was the last speaker that day. The 500 seat hall only had 110 people left. I bribed them to stay with a prize. Everyone remaining at the end went home with a Timpson discount card.

It's flattering when people come forward at the finish to congratulate you. Don't be fooled. Most are consultants waving their business cards hoping you will pay them money to teach you about the topic you have just spoken about. Once, a man from a speaker's agency offered me coaching to improve my presentation.

A few weeks ago I went to a wedding where our son Edward was best man. We were separated from the young and put at a grey haired table which produced some lively conversation. There were two other public speakers – one a professor, the other a minor celebrity on the women's luncheon club circuit. I was fascinated to find they also had days of disaster. The professor was invited to speak to a government department but security wouldn't let him in the building, and the celebrity turned up to talk at Ashford in Kent when she should have been at Ashford in Middlesex. We agreed on some basic guidelines - don't be the last speaker of the day and refuse to join a panel answering questions from the audience.

My worst experience was on a panel in the middle of Earls Court. The conference was part of an exhibition. We fought to be heard against the hubbub outside, not helped by Mickey Mouse microphones. An audience of 150 was expected, but only 57 arrived and 23 quickly disappeared because they could hardly hear. When I stood up, the audience had dwindled to 21. One was asleep and the other 20 were probably consultants. It was a total disaster, but the chairman summed up saying it was wonderful, the sleeper awoke and rushed forward with his business card.

"At least," I said to my new found colleagues at the wedding, "my speaking gets our name known round the country."

"I didn't catch what you did," said the professor. "Timpson" I said, "a national chain of service shops." "Never heard of them," he replied.

Customers

A cornerstone of Timpson's success has been the quality of the service that it provides to its customers. Here is no empty lip service; no empowerment-filled jargon about customer relationship management. It's about well-trained, pleasant, motivated individuals treating every single customer who walks into a shop in the way that they would like to be treated themselves. It's easily said, but all too rarely well done. Here's a flavour of how and why it actually happens.

13

Get someone else to do it

I have been severely criticised for my recent articles. The complaints came from my wife Alex. "All you talk about is disaster," she said. "People will think you are surrounded by chaos. Why not produce some good news for once?" By chance, the same day, this letter came:

"Dear Mr Timpson,

I thought I ought to write and tell you about the wonderful service I have received at your shop in Leamington Spa. I had a bunch of 15 keys cut at another of your branches in the Birmingham area and one didn't work. Your Leamington Spa staff could not have been more helpful. Not only did they recut the key (which now works perfectly) but they also cut another key for nothing and gave me £2 towards my petrol and parking. I will certainly be using your shops again.

Yours etc.

I was thinking about the letter the following Friday while waiting at the supermarket check-out. Gherkins were the problem. I was guilty of picking up a jar without a bar code. Before I could say "they're 36p," the check-out girl rang her bell and waved my gherkins in the air. A young man took the gherkins on a gentle stroll to the other side of the store and returned with the news that they were indeed 36p. If only they had believed me, we could have been saved five minutes and a lot of bother.

My gherkins were trouble-free compared with Kerry's swedes. Kerry, our training supervisor, was shopping at his local Sainsbury's when he spotted a special offer – "free swedes if you buy 5lb of potatoes." Kerry had plenty of potatoes in stock, but he is passionate about swedes. He took a packet of swedes to the check-out. "Where are the potatoes?" said the assistant. "I don't want potatoes, I just want swedes." "But you can't have them without the potatoes," said the assistant. "I'll pay for the swedes," said Kerry. "You can't pay for them, they're free," said the assistant. "But I don't want them for nothing! You tell me how much they are and I'll pay for the swedes." "Sorry, can't do that." Exasperated, Kerry found a supervisor who allowed him to buy the swedes for the price of a packet of potatoes.

In 1975, when I was a very young chief executive, I wrote "10 Golden Rules of Service" in an attempt to improve our level of customer care. The Rules were announced in a blaze of internal publicity and communicated through a nationwide training programme. The result was poor: we only achieved a small improvement in customer service. It took me years to discover the service secret. If you want to look after customers, don't lay down rules. Give your staff freedom. A service business must delegate.

The problem isn't confined to shops. Try getting a call centre to bend the rules. Last year my daughter was working in New Zealand.

Her credit card was near its limit and as she was going on a short holiday to Tahiti, she asked me if I could bring her account back to base. I rang the credit card company who stated the usual, "we can only talk to the account holder." I explained that my daughter was in New Zealand and I wanted to clear the debit balance. "We can't divulge details of your daughter's account," they said. I explained the emergency trip to Tahiti and asked to speak to the supervisor. I had a similar conversation with the supervisor and moved on to her supervisor. I tried a new tactic: "I'm not asking for her balance," I said. "I just want to clear her account. If I put in £400 would that be enough?" "No" was the reply. "How about £600?" "No." "£850?" "That might nearly do it." "I'll send you a cheque for £900." "That will be fine."

I now so passionately believe the way to good customer service is through delegation that I am putting up a notice in all our shops. "The staff in this shop have my total authority to do whatever they think will best give you an amazing service."

The most difficult part of delegation is dealing with the middle management. They are reluctant to relinquish power and find it difficult to believe that anyone else can do a job as well as they can. But we're gradually getting the message across. I keep telling them that good managers know how to stand back and watch everyone else have a go.

I showed this article to Alex before submitting it. "That's better. At least the disasters are in other companies instead of your own," she said. "But tell me something. If you're so keen on delegation, why have you got to work this weekend?" "It's nothing really," I replied. "I'm just drafting a leaflet about the new immobiliser car keys."

Alex was unimpressed. "So you have 850 people working for you, you believe in delegation and you're going to spend half the weekend drafting a leaflet about immobiliser car keys. Why don't you let someone else do it?" "Well to be honest," I replied, "It's easier to do it myself."

14

Forget-me-nots

It's not easy being a cobbler. I was sitting next to a smart young lawyer at a dinner party the other day, when he launched into a favourite old story.

"I suppose you have heard the one about the man who returned from the war?" he said. I knew it only too well. "He found an old shoe repair ticket in his pocket and took it back to the shoe repairer who, to his surprise, had his shoes sitting on the shelf." I prepared a polite giggle for the punchline. "The cobbler turned to the soldier and said 'they'll be ready for next Tuesday'."

My trade might be very much old economy and a bit of a joke, but at least we provide a useful service. And we do it while you wait. Take my mother-in-law. She gets a completely personal service – I take her shoes to the office for repair at a local shop. Last week, for example, she gave me her favourite walking shoes to be mended by Friday. What could be more personal than that?

That Friday was going to be chase-up day. I had a big list but Barbara my secretary got in first. "Can you ring Bill?" (He's a local solicitor.) "He needs to speak to you urgently." I got his voicemail. "This is Bill Tomkinson on Friday September 15. I am not at my desk but if you leave a message I will come straight back to you."

I rang Andrew, a pleasant guy but totally unreliable. We were trying to arrange a meeting but he said he needed a week to sort out his diary. "I guarantee to give you a ring next week." (That was over a fortnight ago). I got Andrew's answerphone. "Sorry, I am not available at the moment, please leave a message after the bleep or try my mobile 0468..."

I rang the mobile. "This is the answering service for 0468... Please leave a message after the tone."

During the next two hours I heard recorded message after recorded message. Whenever I did actually talk to a real person I was fobbed off with a thinly fabricated response. "Your letter is in front of me but I haven't been able to give it enough thought... It's got to go to the board and they don't meet for three weeks... Your proposal is with my director but he has just gone on holiday."

I gave Bill Tomkinson another ring. "This is Bill Tomkinson on Friday September 15. I am not at my desk but if you leave a message I will come straight back to you."

I was just wondering whether I should abandon the office and go to the driving range, when my wife Alex rang. "Have you forgotten about the septic tank? You promised to get someone to check it out," she said. "I did it three weeks ago, I thought the job had been done." I rang the septic tank man immediately. His wife answered the phone. Sid's been ill and he is up to his eyes in it, you're scheduled for next week." Fed up, I said I'd get someone else to do it. Strangely, Sid suddenly became available.

But delay and false promises are not confined to business. Tony Blair is no better. On May 3, I wrote to the prime minister with a couple of pointers to help his campaign on adoption. My letter was acknowledged after six weeks and the reply arrived on July 15. I mentioned this delay to a politically aware friend who thought I was lucky to get such a speedy reply.

I worried whether this national epidemic of inertia had spread into my own business. I went to check our most critical area, customer complaints.

When customers write to complain, a quick response is vital. The results of my own investigation were favourable. On average, we reply within 48 hours and the longest anyone waits is five days.

With a feeling of smug contentment I drove home. My mobile rang as soon as I got in the car. It was the answerphone service. "You have one new message." It was my friend Gordon. He couldn't play golf on Wednesday because he was playing in Spain instead. I rang Gordon and he answered the phone after two rings. Within 30 seconds we had rearranged the date for October 17. No hassle, no phoning back, no messages. So simple. Why can't life always be as easy as that?

Before I got home, I was in for a shock. The phone rang again. "Bill Tomkinson here. Just returning your call." At least the week ended on a positive note.

On Sunday, mother-in-law came for lunch as usual, and as soon as I saw her face coming through the door, an image flashed into my mind. Her walking boots were still sitting, unrepaired, on the back seat of my car.

"John," said Alex. "Have you got those shoes repaired for my mother?" "Oh yes, I haven't forgotten," I said. "Just proving a bit more difficult than I expected, they'll be ready for next Tuesday."

15

Many Complaints

"Have you ever wondered how they got there?" commented Alex as I took a perfectly ironed shirt out of my wardrobe. "I have got an interesting day," I said, pretending not to hear. "Peter wants to take me through some problems he has with customer complaints." "I thought your customer care was wonderful," said Alex sarcastically. "Have you learned at last that even people as perfect as you can make mistakes?"

Handling complaints has been a favourite hobby ever since I used it as a weapon against my main competitor in the seventies. British Shoe Corporation, the Sears' subsidiary that once enjoyed over 20 per cent of the retail footwear market, had a draconian way of dealing with complaining customers. Shop staff had to keep complaints below three per cent of sales. If they reached this limit, all further complainers were turned away dissatisfied.

I cleaned up our complaints policy and turned it into a television commercial that announced: "If you have good reason to be dissatisfied with our shoes, we will give you your money back, and that's a promise." British Shoe's chief executive said my campaign was like giving petrol to an arsonist, but I still booked the advertising and prepared for a public relations campaign.

I was grilled by a PR consultant who taught me how to tackle tricky TV interviewers. He tested me with some trial questions. "Aren't you ashamed," he asked me, "that 2,000 pairs of your shoes fall to bits every week?" "That's unfair," I replied. "You don't mention the 100,000 which are absolutely fine." "Wrong answer," he told me firmly. "Never try and sweep your problems under the carpet. You should have said, 'you're right, we still have problems, but our complaints policy shows we are keen to tackle them. There is no cause for complacency'."

Barbara was waiting for me when I arrived at the office. "Before you see Peter about his complaints problems, you have one of your own. Remember you wrote to the airline following your delayed flight back from holiday? They have sent a letter at last." "Is it three weeks since I complained ?" I asked. "No, four," said Barbara, "and you haven't got a reply now. It's a standard letter saying your complaint has been referred to the customer service manager who is on holiday." "Typical," I said. "They should have our system which gives everyone individual authority to settle complaints, with no need to refer to an area manager or customer service director."

Barbara raised her eyebrows as I proudly launched into my complaints policy. "In our business any customer with a problem can be dealt with straight away. We know it's impossible to make sure every key we cut works, but complaints give us an excellent chance to amaze our customers. Good staff not only recut the key but give customers a spare and pay for their car parking." "Before you get too complacent," said Barbara, "you had better speak to Peter, I get the impression your complaints procedure is not as perfect as you think."

Peter got straight to the point. "It's getting worse." he said. "Last year we got 20 letters a week, now it's 30. Britain is becoming a nation of complainers and it's not fair on Joan who speaks to the people on the telephone. Before long she will be off with stress. I don't mind justified complaints but look at some of these we have received today. I will start with Mr Pilkington from Peckham who should be called 'Mr Angry.' He says we have ruined his shoes by using the wrong kind of sole; I have offered to give a full refund and do the job again for free, but all he does is shout at me down the phone. Then there is John Tiffin from Kent who insists on his consumer rights. He says a man on the market cuts keys for £2 and we should charge the same. He says it's a scandal and is reporting us to Trading Standards. My worst nightmare is Sheila Saunders who lives in Shropshire. I feel I know her as well as my own family, she's never off the 'phone. I'm convinced she is addicted to complaining. Every time I ask her what we can do to make things right, she never replies, she doesn't want the complaint satisfied, she just wants to whinge. The final straw was this letter from a solicitor, dealing with the will of a woman who was the widow of one of our pensioners. Among her possessions he found a £5 discount voucher dated 1989. He wanted us to send him the £5 so he could add it to the estate, he labelled the letter 'urgent' as our fiver was needed before he could submit the final accounts."

Thank goodness I had something to brighten Peter's day. "You must have missed this letter when you went through your post," I said. It was from Mrs Harvey in Harrogate, writing in glowing terms about Peter. "He is a credit to your company," she wrote. "He handled my complaint so well, I only expected to receive the cost of my key but Peter went much further. You have a very satisfied customer." Peter was satisfied too - he left my office a much happier man.

That night I was changing to go out for dinner, when I saw a crease in the shirt I had just removed from the wardrobe. I pointed it out to Alex. Her comment: "Trust you to complain, you don't mentioned the 50,000 shirts I iron perfectly."

Personal Productivity

Few business people have gone on the record as honestly as John about their frustrations – not just with other people, or institutions, but with themselves. How many other chief executives can cheerfully confess to having achieved next to nothing in a working day, or losing important papers? The flip side, of course, is a man who is relentlessly good at getting things done.

16

The big to-do

I was just leaving the house early last Monday morning when my wife Alex shouted from upstairs, "can you bring back some red polish for the children's shoes?"

I played a 7.30am game of tennis before a busy day at the office. As well as the monthly board meeting, I recorded a video for our new company training programme. I walked round the office for half an hour, made four phone calls. I scribbled some hand-written notes to shops that had had a good week and on the way home called to see an aunt who lives on her own.

The sales figures had been good and I was keen to tell Alex about the successes of the day. I was taken aback by the first question as I walked through the door – "have you got the red polish?"

As far as Alex was concerned, my successful day had been a complete failure. I had failed to put the polish on my list.

Immediately, I took my briefcase to the study and added red polish at the bottom of the A4 pad which contained all the other things that needed to be done.

The list would have meant little to anybody who tried to pry into my paperwork. I use a few short words to remind me of each task. Immediately above where I had written red polish were the following notes:

- N.A. floor.
- Timberland News.
- Gareth £300.
- Yates' Wine.
- Helen chest waxing.

I had better explain how such a bizarre collection of items is relevant to running a chain of shoe repair and key-cutting shops.

- **N.A. floor.** The shopfitters had left the floor behind our watch-repair unit in Newton Abbot on a distinct slant. The poor watch-repairer who has a stool with wheels keeps sliding back towards the window.

- **Timberland News.** Our specialist shoe repair factory provides a service for the Timberland brand. I want our sales team to create a regular newsletter to Timberland stockists promoting this service.

- **Gareth £300.** Gareth, a shop manager, lives in a flat with no facility to park his car. He wants to borrow £300 from the company to purchase the materials to create a hard core area. I need to make arrangements to lend the money.

- **Yates' Wine.** The other day I walked past Yates' Wine Lodge in Chester and thought their displays would work well in part of our shop. I need to talk to our marketing director. (Not difficult as he is my son James!!)

- **Helen chest waxing.** Bob Northover, our manager in Taunton, is having his chest waxed to raise money for the NSPCC. A local beauty parlour will be doing the deed in four weeks' time. Helen looks after my public relations. I need to let her know so she can contact the local papers.

Of course the best way to avoid forgetting is to do things straight away. But even with a mobile phone you can't do everything immediately, so a notepad is my constant companion.

At the end of each day, I transfer scribbled notes onto an A4 pad adding any vital tasks that Alex might want to include.

For the first four years I turned a list into action by starting at the top and going steadily through until I reached the bottom. As a result, I contacted the same people on several different occasions as I worked my rigid chronological way down the list of items. I now use a different method. I put a name against each item and list all the people involved at the top of the sheet and see them one by one.

I tick each item as it is dealt with, but I don't cross it out. Telling someone does not guarantee that action will be taken. Everything stays on the list until I am certain the job has finally been done. Even then, I don't throw my list away.

Every three or four months I have a clear-out. I go through all the old lists and create a new schedule of things remaining to be done and ideas that are still important. They are rearranged under headings: key cutting, shoe repairs, watch repairs and marketing. This process always reveals one or two of my pet ideas that have been totally ignored by everyone else in the business.

By now you will know that my list-making is an obsession. But it works. Despite my lousy memory, I have a reputation for never forgetting anything.

This Friday I had one of those days when I achieved absolutely nothing. I flitted from one task to another, was interrupted by unproductive phone calls and spent 20 minutes looking for a piece of paper that was right in front of me.

It was an entirely useless day until I looked at my A4 pad. Despite the apparent disorganisation, I had done everything on my list. I even managed to arrive home with the tin of red polish!

17

Phoneys

Six weeks ago I seriously upset my secretary, Barbara. I instructed our switchboard to put all calls directly through to my office, avoiding Barbara's screening process that has been in operation for 20 years.

I'd had a particularly bad run of abortive phone calls – calling people who wouldn't speak to me. Whoever I rang was either out of the office, in a meeting or on voicemail.

Requests to ring back went unanswered. So I tried again. The person who was out of the office had popped back but had now gone into a meeting. The person who was in a meeting was now in another meeting and the voicemail message had changed to tell me my man had gone on holiday.

It is worth using charm to try and cut through the secretarial security net – "could he possibly break away from the meeting for a few moments?" I have, however, found that a small white lie brings more immediate results. Try: "I was just ringing to discuss the possibility of placing a £1m order" or "I have been asked to ring by Downing Street regarding the Honours List." But I don't see why I must use such devious tactics just to have a word on the phone.

I cannot help wondering what all these meetings are about. What are they discussing and who is there? You see, I myself don't have many meetings. There is a formal board meeting once a month, and everything else is not much more than a series of conversations to discuss how the business is going.

Very occasionally, I might be discussing a personal matter which I wouldn't like to have interrupted, but most of the time I am happy to be disturbed. I have two exceptions: I won't take calls if I have got a visitor from outside the business (such as a supplier or the bank manager); and I never welcome internal calls.

We operate in a pretty small office (10,000 sq ft). It takes me no more than 40 seconds to walk to any part of the building. I never make an internal call – I always walk to meet the person face-to-face. I expect everybody else to do the same.

I have noticed that the people you can't get hold of often work for unsuccessful businesses. It may mean that trading problems cause more meetings to be held, but it could be that the problems are made worse by having senior executives spending all their time tied up in meetings.

Please don't run away with the idea that I think you can run a business without meeting people. Quite the reverse. Good communication is essential and the best contact is face-to-face. I don't see why meetings should be used as a screen to protect executives from the outside world. That's why I decided to carry out my experiment. As soon as I had mentioned the plan to the switchboard, my phone started to ring.

"Don't say I didn't warn you," said Barbara.

I enjoyed the unsolicited calls from telesales people. Previously they had taken up quite a lot of time without me speaking to them.

75

Salesmen are very expert at getting through the secretary net posing as personal friends, or saying they are returning my call. Even Barbara sometimes has difficulty spotting the genuine caller.

"Do you know George Zimmerman?" says Barbara. "He says he knows you." "I can't remember his name. What does he want to talk about?" I ask. "He won't tell me," says Barbara. They never do.

By the time Barbara and I have discussed whether the caller could be an old business colleague or school friend, a distant member of the family, or someone who has got a genuine cause to speak to me, I might just as well have taken the call myself.

I have never had any problem dealing with salesmen on the telephone. It's easy because I always know the answer. Whether I am being offered special hotel deals, a hospitality box at Ascot, vital consultancy advice, or an opportunity to advertise in the police gazette, the answer is always no.

I have reduced the average time of these calls to around four seconds. It is not fair to waste time when the caller could move on to another punter that might produce a sale and some commission. There is no need to be aggressive; a little bit of a smile in the voice helps. I just say, "before you go any further, I would just like you to know that I am not interested." I never have to put the phone down; they put the phone down on me.

Yes, Barbara had warned me. The third phone call I received gave me a hint of what she was saying. It was my wife Alex. "Oh, I didn't want you," she said. "I wanted to speak to Barbara."

The next call was from David Mawson, my financial adviser. "Isn't Barbara in?" he said. "It was her I was trying to get hold of."

By the time I had received three more such calls, I got the message. For the last 20 years, Barbara has been running the office, not me. Shortly after lunch I called my new scheme to a halt and the switchboard reverted to putting all calls through to Barbara.

You can still speak to me; Barbara knows that I like to receive as many external calls as possible. But we have a board meeting on the third Monday of every month. So if you ring between 10am and 1pm on that day, Barbara will tell you, "he's in a meeting."

18

Has anyone seen my desk?

Important papers have a nasty habit of disappearing from my office. One day, I was reading a long-awaited report on complicated keys when the telephone went. It was one of our shop managers ringing to tell me about a record week. He went on to ask me to supply free end-of-season trophies to his local boys' Sunday football league. By the time I had congratulated him on his recent successes and agreed to donate some trophies, the key technology report had vanished.

After a ten-minute search, I found the report hiding under the daily cash statement, which I was about to put in the wastepaper basket when the telephone rang. Having found the report, I couldn't read it. I had lost my glasses. Someone had cleverly lodged them within the curls of my telephone flex. This was no isolated incident. I probably spend an hour each week looking for spectacles, my diary and missing papers. I decided to do something, so I had a word with Barbara, my secretary. "I can't stand all this paper," I started.

"This isn't as bad as most other offices in this building," countered Barbara, who'd already worked out that a spring clean would mean moving most of the paper out of my office into her office with a suggestion that she "filed anything important."

I always listen to Barbara so, before taking action, I toured the building. As usual, she was right. The property director has used up all the available shelf and desk space and now piles files on the floor – "a lot going on right now," he explained, "all these files relate to live issues."

Next to the managing director. No files on the floor here. His thing was to keep back numbers of management magazines neatly arranged in four-foot skyscrapers. My finance director is not a particularly tall man and it was difficult to see him behind the mound of paper on his desk. He was compiling a report on paperwork savings for the next board meeting. I decided not to ask the obvious question and moved on.

I was nearly fooled by our training manager. His desk was absolutely clear, apart from a proud display of training manuals. He keeps his office paper-free by stuffing everything into one of 15 filing cabinets that occupy the space of a sixties mainframe computer. Talking of computers, you shouldn't be surprised to hear that the IT manager won my prize for the "paper-full office." Most of it was produced by the computer that I thought we had bought to get rid of paper altogether.

Barbara was right, a lot of offices were worse than mine but some were better. Of the two best, one was a big surprise. When my son James lived at our house, you could hardly get into his room for clutter. But on my tour of inspection, James' office was a paper-free zone. He told me the secret. "I have a simple rule. I only look at things once. After reading a document, I throw it away." And he was throwing things away in some style – using a large cardboard carton as a wastepaper basket. On top of his carton, I noticed the screwed-up remains of some useful ideas I had sent him that morning!

Our display manager won the prize. He had just had a spring clean and looked very smug as a result. I decided to take a leaf out of his book. I was just going on holiday and in the mood for a massive clear-out. I didn't bother to ask Barbara, I just got on with it and frankly I enjoyed the experience. I invented a second rule. I gave myself two seconds to decide whether each document was kept, filed or thrown away. There was no time to read any of the papers, so I wasn't diverted from the main task. If in doubt, I threw things out safe in the knowledge that the training manager keeps a copy of everything. The whole exercise was a great success. I cleared my office, Barbara got lots of filing, and I went on holiday.

While I was relaxing in my deckchair on the Algarve, I started to wonder what had happened to the paperless office. Perhaps people do prefer the telephone to an e-mail; an A4 pad to a laptop.

After a week's thought in the sun, I came to a conclusion.

I find out more during a day visiting our shops than I discover from a monthly supply of memos. All this paper is getting in the way. The more there is to read, the less time I have to get out of the office. The case for cutting out paper is overwhelming. I came back from holiday with a clear plan. Friday 13 was looming and I was going to declare it "Paper Purge Day." I planned to issue everybody with a carton just like the one James uses to clear his desk.

The flight home was delayed. Alec from the office picked the family up at the airport. He had put three large briefcases in the boot of my car, filled – you've guessed it – with paperwork!

I didn't have time to put my ideas into practice straight away. Friday 13 came and went and then I got involved in a possible acquisition that eventually fell through. I was starting to look forward to my next holiday when it happened again. I lost an important report on our locksmith business. After a record 20-minute search, it was found hiding under the daily cash report I was about to put into the wastepaper basket.

19

One quick question...

I had achieved next to nothing by 4pm last Tuesday, when Barbara came into my office. "You haven't forgotten that *Real Business* needs another article by the end of the week?" "I know," I replied. "That's another thing I haven't done today. I just can't do anything in the office." "You decided to have an open door policy," Barbara reminded me. "Point taken," I admitted, "but it would be nice to have some peace and quiet with time to think." "Why not spend a day at home?" said Barbara. "Clear up your unfinished jobs and return to the office with a smile on your face." Sounded like a great idea to me. Alex was not quite so pleased. "Do you realise it's half-term and the decorators are here.

What's the problem, no-one speaking to you at the office?" Undeterred by this cool reception, I looked forward to Tuesday. Never mind the decorators, I could lock myself away in my study – six uninterrupted hours of solitude. It was bliss not driving to the office. I cooked bacon and egg, which I ate while reading the newspaper. "If you've got time to sit around, why not take the dog for a walk?" said Alex. So I did, and enjoyed it, listening to the commuter traffic in the distance while I walked in the winter sunshine. As I returned, Alex was driving off to the shops. "Before you start, can you reply to the three invitations that have been hanging around since last week? I'll be back in two hours." I wrote the letters in no time and even had some stamps on my desk. It was a brilliant start to what promised to be a very efficient day.

I needed to finish a speech for next week's company dinner. I looked for the notes in my briefcase. They weren't there, I must have left them at the office. I rang Barbara. "No problem," she said "They are where you left them on a chair by your desk. I'll send them on the fax." The sun was still shining so I walked to the post box, but no fax welcomed my return. I rang Barbara. "Have you sent the notes?" "I tried several times, but it won't go through." Just then I saw the words "paper jam." "Someone has been using my fax," I told Barbara. "Try again in a few minutes." I pushed the paper in and out, but the machine was still jammed. I remembered my foolproof way to fix the fax. I switched off the mains, and switched on again. I rang Barbara to tell her it was working.

The telephone rang. "Who's that?" said the voice at the other end. "Oh it's you, what are you doing at home today?" I recognised the voice, it was a local builder. "Is Mrs Timpson there?" "No, but she'll be back soon. Can I help?" "No, I'll ring back."While I was on the phone, the fax arrived. At last I could write my speech. I'd just sat down to start when the phone rang again. It was Barbara. "Just ringing to see whether the fax has arrived." There was a knock on the study door. Alex brought some tea. "I've organised a babysitter so I'm free for lunch. I'm sure you'll need a break in an hour. In the meantime, I'll be outside." Five minutes later, the phone rang again. "What number is that?" said a friend of Alex's, astounded that a man had answered. "It's the Timpson residence." "Oh I want to speak to Alex." "Hang on I'll look for her in the garden."On my way back from the greenhouse, Geoff the decorator asked whether I could spare five minutes, he had a business problem. I was happy to help. Half an hour later I was more baffled than Geoff. He was trying to complete his tax return. Thank goodness I have a finance director.

We were still wrestling with his problem when Alex came in. "You've done enough for one morning, it's 12.45." We had a leisurely lunch at the Grosvenor Arms and it was 3pm before I was back in my study. Peace at last, certainly much quieter than the office. I had just finished writing the speech when Barbara rang again. "Can you contact George urgently, there's a problem with the new shop in Swindon". "Glad you rang," I said, "I am putting the finished speech on the fax, could you type it for tomorrow?" George didn't have a problem, he just wanted a chat. He went on for 25 minutes. As soon as I put the phone down it rang again. It was Barbara. "The fax has arrived – have you forgotten the article for *Real Business*?" "No Barbara, I'll start it now." But I didn't, I made myself a cup of tea, switched on the television and watched Countdown followed by The Weakest Link.

I made an early start the following day to beat the traffic through Birmingham. But failed. I spent two hours in a traffic jam with nothing else to do but write this article for *Real Business*.

20

i'll call U L8R

I was watching Top of the Pops to see if I could distinguish Westlife from Hear'Say and Shaggy from Cher when Henry, my teenage son, looked up from his Gameboy to ask a surprisingly intelligent question. "What invention has done most to improve your life?" I was shocked into serious thought.

The computer is the obvious answer. Everyone said I would notice computers at the millennium when the bug struck, but apart from Alex insisting I shopped for a siege, filling six trolleys at Sainsbury's, computers didn't change my life.

I considered the internet, but I have not seriously gone online. I will do soon. Most of my retired friends go on a computer course and tell me the internet is marvellous.

I was tempted to choose motorways. They would have made an enormous difference but the government stopped building them. I thought of the microwave because it saves so much time, but convenience food stops us meeting our families round a dinner table.

I made up my mind. In my opinion, the most helpful invention is the mobile phone. It lets me spend lots of time out of the office. "How can you say that?" said Henry, "when you always slag off mobiles?"

"It's other people's phones that are annoying, not mine. I don't take my mobile into someone else's office. I don't use it at restaurants. It doesn't ring out with the William Tell overture (or Shaggy's latest hit). I even have the courage to complain to offenders in the quiet coach on Virgin rail."

"But if you think the mobile is so useful," countered Henry, "why can't I ever get hold of you?"

The mobile has been a car phone to me ever since I first acquired one in 1980. I was a pioneer. The contraption was as big as a briefcase and as heavy as a pile of bricks. On the rare occasions it was in range of a signal, I was one of the first to use the now familiar phrases, "You are very faint: You are cracking up: Are you still there?" It was too heavy to throw down in a rage, so I relieved my anger by kicking the thing, which sometimes brought it back to life. That phone seldom worked, but it got me out of the office.

After such an early start, I failed to keep up with developments. Last September an area manager was helping me reprogramme my favourite numbers following a dialling code change, when he noticed I had received my first text message. It was from my daughter, sending best wishes for Father's Day – three months before.

I don't take my mobile into public places. You won't find me bellowing business-speak while walking down Bond Street. It's getting worse. In the last fortnight I have heard phones ringing at an organ recital, on the first green at Hoylake and, worst of all, someone held up a supermarket queue when her boyfriend rang. The person with the phone was the check-out girl.

The doorbell rang and two friends arrived to take Henry for a night out. "Just going for a couple of beers," he said. "Back before 11." He had got me thinking. Other people's phones are a pain, and it's going to get worse. Tony Blair is determined we should all embrace new technology; it's his secret weapon in creating "the new Britain." Perhaps he is pleased with the way we ring mum from the supermarket to check whether she wants medium or thick sliced bread. Maybe he is delighted that his school-age subjects send text messages to classmates at the back of the bus.

And phones are getting smaller – soon we will be wearing them on our wrists. Before long it might be compulsory. The mobile could become an electronic identity card: link them to GPS and the government will not only know who you are, but where you are. You won't be able to claim that you're stuck in a traffic jam when the caller can work out that you're still in the pub.

We are bound to see progress, whether we want it or not. Someone will try to recover those billions spent on the 3G licences, and the Carphone Warehouse will still want to sell more phones even though everyone has one. Soon we will have two mobiles, one on each wrist. "Sorry, can you hang on, I am on the left-hand line." Each phone will have a television screen so you can see the caller. I can't wait to see the secretary's face when she says her boss is in a meeting. You could hold a conference call on the 6.55 from Crewe to Euston. I am sure no-one will mind as long as you avoid the quiet coach.

And with these new devices linked to the internet, we will have the Encyclopedia Britannica, the Stock Exchange and Sky Sports available with a flick of the wrist. New technology will provide so much fun and information that there will be little time left for work. But who cares? We mustn't stand in the way of progress.

Suddenly, I realised it was 11.30pm and there was no sign of Henry. I rang his mobile, but there was no reply. Where was he? Had he been mugged, was he in a car crash? When he walked through the door, I hugged him first, then anger took over. "Why didn't you take your mobile phone?"

21

I'm not in

A few weeks ago after Sunday lunch, I set off with my son James to walk the dogs so we could talk about business without being told off. "It's amazing what people say on the phone," said James. "A man rang me from Florida on Friday saying he could generate a 20 per cent saving on all our costs. When I asked how he could cut our rent, he said he would renegotiate our leases, so I suggested he could always cut our staffing levels by closing a few shops. He said I was being sarcastic."

"How did you get him off the phone?" I asked.

"I used the usual routine," said James. "I transferred the call to the finance department."

I know how James feels. We seem to spend more and more of our lives being pestered by salesmen. I had a bellyful on a recent visit to Bath. While walking 250 yards down the main street, I had to side-step four Big Issue salesmen, two buskers and three bold girls with green bibs who wanted me to sign a standing order for Barnados. I avoided the man who wanted to know if I had had an accident at work but got collared by the market researcher who stopped me to ask whether I could spare five minutes to talk about headache pills.

I have avoided street interviews ever since Alex was questioned in the centre of Chester, having been tempted by the offer of a free holiday. Soon after, she received a telephone call inviting her to claim the prize at a drinks party near Lancaster. Curiosity took us up the M6 to a holiday park just off the motorway. We were given tea, biscuits and the undivided attention of a time-share salesman, who explained that for one signature and a substantial deposit, we could secure a week's holiday anywhere in the world for the rest of our lives. When I asked to see his company accounts, he quickly ended the interview, and ushered us off the premises.

After James and I returned with the dogs, the phone rang. "I have good news for you," said a young girl reading from a script. "Your kitchen has been chosen for a makeover. If you agree to let us use pictures of the finished job in our publicity, all the work will be half-price. You will save at least £5,000."

"Sorry to disappoint you. We have just redone our kitchen," I said and put the phone down.

"Let's have a competition," suggested James, "to see who can create the quickest and politest way to get unwanted salesmen off the phone."

At the office the following morning, Barbara looked impatient as she held the telephone six inches from her ear. I pointed to myself to ask whether the call was for me. Barbara waved me away. A minute later she popped her head in the office. "I've got this man on the phone called Roberts," she said. "He says he knows you, but he won't say where he is from or what he wants to talk about. "Oh, put him through," I said, seizing the chance to test a technique that could win the competition.

"Do you want to improve your bottom line?" said the man.

"I am," I replied.

"Well done, but would you like to identify where you still have excess expenses? We can normally find 20 per cent."

"One cost I can't cut is consultancy," I responded. "We don't use them. If you have something to offer, please put it in writing. Sorry I must go, there is someone at the door."

The next call was put straight through to my office. "Hi John," he said. "It's Chris from California. I am in your area next week and wondered if I could drop by."

"Look," I interrupted, "next week is already fully booked."

"But…" he started. "No, I am sorry," I said firmly. "I don't have time to see you."

I went to James' office to tell him how I had successfully rebuffed two callers. He was talking to a man selling corporate hospitality packages for the Commonwealth Games. "I think you have the wrong number," said James. "I run a cobbler's shop. Hang on a minute, I am going to have to go, there is a customer coming through the door." I was clearly losing our competition.

The following Sunday we were walking the dogs again. "Some people are so rude on the phone," said James. He had spent a day working with our new venture, Keys Direct. It offers businesses a key-management system that saves them a lot of time and money. James worked with one of our salesmen, cold calling on the phone. "All I asked," said James, "was whether they wanted help with their key problems and to save money at the same time. Five in a row said 'I don't talk to salesmen', and put the phone down."

Alex overheard us as we walked into the yard. "Not talking business again, are you?" "No," I lied. "James was telling me about a telephone call he made last week."

"That reminds me," said Alex. "Did that nice Chris ever get hold of you? You know, the guy from California that we met on holiday, who you were so keen to do business with. He rang here the other day to see if he could come and stay, but as you organise the diary these days, I asked him to ring you at the office."

22

Why work my fingers to the bone?

"Another busy day at the office I see." said Alex sarcastically, as I furtively emptied my sports bag by the washing machine. Alex has only herself to blame for all that washing; 15 years ago she labelled me a workaholic and actively encouraged alternatives to work. I have been finding them ever since. Golf, tennis, real tennis and squash find a regular slot in my diary and Alex finds sports clothes in the wash at least four times a week. Today I am more likely to get stressed by problems with my golf swing or my forehand than trouble at the office.

That evening, by mistake, Alex picked up an old *Sunday Times* business section. "Are you sure you are not semi-retired?" she said. "I have just been reading this article about a 'captain of industry'. His typical day starts at 5.45am, he eats muesli for breakfast, cycles to the station and is in the office by 7.30am. He spends one hour looking at e-mails, followed by a full round of meetings, rarely breaking for lunch. He spends one day a week visiting a regional office and another meeting contacts in the City. He goes out for dinner every evening, most times connected with business, but makes sure that one night a week, he and his wife can dine alone. Saturday is a family day, but by Sunday lunchtime he is back at work preparing for the week ahead."

I guessed what was coming. "How do you fit in all your sport and still run the business?" asked Alex. I thought of starting a discussion, but there seemed little point. Alex has won every debate that we have had for the last 30 years.

I got up at 5.45 the following morning and arrived at the airport for 6.30am. Several high-flying executives were already sat in Starbucks with their *Financial Times*, laptop and mobile phone. Who are they phoning at 6.30 in the morning? Perhaps they are calling one of those merchant bankers who works seven days a week. I sometimes wonder, maybe unfairly, whether such long hours are really necessary. Has work become an end in itself or have they, as I did, become workaholics?

On the aeroplane I squeezed my 15-stone frame into a Twiggy-sized seat and tried to fold a newspaper without disturbing my neighbour. I opened it up to another story about a big businessman's working day.

This one starts with a dawn jog round Dulwich before being driven into the City at 7am. He spends the journey phoning Far Eastern colleagues from the car, then when he arrives at his glass and pine-wood office, he checks his e-mails. His day follows the time zones. In the morning he talks to Europe, in the afternoon he contacts North America. He stays in the office until 7pm. Once home, he swallows a quick bite before catching up with any e-mails he missed at the office.

When I first became a managing director, 27 years ago, we employed a smart fresh-faced young man who had been singled out as a future star. He was a hard worker, always the last to leave the office.

One night I forgot my briefcase, and went back to the office to find my young champion had gone. The caretaker confirmed that the keen young star always left minutes after me.

Our new recruits are given a whirlwind tour on their first day. They are nervously brought into my office to be introduced. One plucky young girl asked me a question. "What does the chairman do?" She probably noticed that everyone else looked busier than me. I couldn't tell her the chairman played lots of golf and tennis, so I gave a limp response about looking after company strategy and communication, and sent her on her way without admitting to the ten weeks of holiday I have planned for this year.

I am growing rather fond of this semi-retired tag, particularly as I feel that I achieve much more now than I did when I worked longer hours. Put another way, the less time I spend with the business, the more successful it seems to become.

Years ago, I learned a lesson during a visit to our Inverness branch. The shop was full of repair work. Boots and shoes were everywhere, more than I had seen at any other branch, and yet the turnover was poor. The manager was taking in lots of work but not taking the money because he didn't get on with the job. Nothing was done "While You Wait." The more the work piled up, the more complicated his life became.

We encourage our shops to do jobs "While You Wait." It makes work a lot easier. The same principle applies in the office. "Do it now" is my top tip for office efficiency. It has taken me 41 years to discover how to save time. As well as "doing it now," I file everything in the waste paper basket, avoid meetings and refuse most conferences and corporate hospitality.

Giving up these "pleasures" has created time for me to think, which is what I was doing when Alex walked into my study to find me staring into space. "I am surprised you are not on the golf course," she said. "If you have nothing better to do, perhaps you can take the dog for a walk."

23

Which bit of your life gets your best attention?

Last year I was invited to a day at ASDA head office. As the *Sunday Times'* best place to work for in the UK, the supermarket chain was entertaining other companies in the *Sunday Times'* top ten for a day designed to demonstrate how they pamper employees. The guests arrived with a mixture of envy and scepticism determined to discover why ASDA topped the list.

ASDA had copied Wal-Mart before Wal-Mart acquired ASDA. They called every worker "a colleague" and made them wear enormous badges on their breast, telling the world "I am here to help."

We were welcomed by the ASDA champion greeter, a big man with a big smile and a very big badge. After he bellowed his Butlin's-style welcome, we obediently filed into the lecture theatre to be formally greeted by people director, David Smith.

"Let's start with an ice breaker," he said. My heart sank, anticipating forced involvement with the ASDA chant – "give us an A, give us an S etcetera etcetera." Fortunately, the ice breaker didn't make me feel a fool; it made me think. It was an exercise to test work-life balance, a novel measurement of today's trendy topic. We filled segments of a circle with the eight most significant sides of our life.

Anxious to prove that I am not a workaholic, I entered work, holidays, golf, tennis, family, fostering, charity work and writing. I thought this gave an excellent balance and I felt particularly smug when I glanced over my neighbour's shoulder. He wrote work, holidays and family, then struggled. Eventually he added sailing and gardening – lies, judging by his pale complexion – and finished with reading, television and sleep.

We calibrated the segments to indicate the time devoted to each activity. I admitted a quarter of my life was work, a similar amount family, and not quite as much golf. We joined the marks and produced a shape that revealed our life's balance. My neighbour drew an elongated sausage – dominated by work. I produced a rather pleasing squashed circle, which showed such an ideal lifestyle I took it home to show Alex.

She was unimpressed. "Let me show you the truth." She drew a diagram. In her version my elegant small circle had changed into an Aladdin's lamp, with the extreme points labelled work and golf. "Look in your diary," said Alex. "It's full of business and sport."

There was no point in arguing. Alex is the Tiger Woods of the debating chamber. I should have forgotten my work-life balance and brought home a box of chocolates instead.

I left at 6.30am the following morning. "Is this early start part of the better balance in your life?" said Alex. "I am golfing with Gordon at 7.30," I said, proving her point.

"Busy day ahead?" I asked Gordon on the tenth tee, trying to put him off. "Not really," he replied. "Perhaps a bit of gardening or lunch at the club." Gordon never seems to work these days. "Thanks to you," he said.

"Ten years ago, I was the hard worker until you introduced me to playing sport during office hours."

"But you carry it to extremes, Gordon," I protested. "Yes I know," he replied smugly. "Since I sold the business, life is full of golf, shooting and holidays. You don't know what you are missing."

Gordon certainly enjoys himself, but I wouldn't want to find my only worry was my golf swing. Life has been better since I introduced "Upside-Down Management" – our version of what other people call delegation or empowerment. It certainly seems to have worked; I am much happier and the business is making more money. Some people have cruelly pointed out that the less time I spend in the business, the more money it makes. I put it differently: the more authority I give people in the business, the more money they make for me.

"I have some bad news," said Barbara as I walked in the office. "George can't make that meeting tomorrow."

"I don't bloody believe it," I said, "not again, the man's impossible." I was meeting George about a deal he suggested and I now wanted to do. Six weeks ago we agreed to meet as soon as possible, but he had left his electronic personal organiser on the train. A week later he sent an e-mail: "Life's hectic, will give a firm date next week." Three weeks later I tracked him down and fixed the meeting he has now cancelled. "Did he give a reason?" I asked Barbara. "He has double-booked. When his organiser was returned, he found an important meeting on the same date." Reluctantly I agreed to a new date the following week.

"It always happens to me," I said to Barbara. "Calm down," she said, "you will make yourself ill. You are becoming a grumpy old man. You complain about everything, voice mail, e-mails and government interference. You can't stand in the way of progress." I bravely resisted. "I disagree," I said. "Why should I be a slave to modern contraptions?"

Alex greeted me as I took my tennis bag from the car. "Another work-life balance day, I see. Good of you to come home to fill in your quota with the family." She waited until I sat down before talking in a way that told me this is serious.

"I have studied my work-life balance," she said. "I'm stuck here cleaning the house, running a taxi service, providing everyone with food and each evening you expect me to be a cheerful conversationalist. I am introducing a bit of balance into my life. I am visiting my friend Penny in Swansea. Her Doug's off sailing and she has invited me for two nights. I am sure you will enjoy looking after the children, and you are always saying how you would love to do the cooking." The following morning I rang George to change the date of our meeting.

Employment Issues

Regularly voted as one of the country's best companies to work for, Timpson has a proud record as an employer. But life and legislation don't always make it easy. The rising tide of employment law and new directives is a constant – and telling – theme in John's columns. So, too, is the linguistic inflation of the "Human Resources" industry. Timpson, naturally, sticks to having a personnel manager.

24

Dreaming about directives

I was wading through a thick report on health and safety when I felt a cold twinge, the first sign I had caught a virus. There had been a lot going around the office, five with flu in finance and another two in personnel, it was obviously my turn. When I arrived home, Alex was waiting, "Are you alright?" she said. "Barbara says you were foul-tempered at the office today."

I went to bed early, with the papers for next week's board meeting, but I fell asleep reading the property report and then my nightmare started. I was chairing a board meeting. A new non-executive looking exactly like Tony Blair smiled at me. "Can we cover the statutory requirements first?" he asked. "What statutory requirements?" I asked. "The ones in front of you," he said, pointing to three enormous files. The thickest file was labelled "Employment," and listed legislation passed since our last meeting:

- Paid paternity leave increases to six months.
- All staff under 21 must be released each week for a day at the nation-wide network of Lifestyle Training Centres.
- A Retirement Acclimatisation Scheme gives every employee over 45 years old, two extra weeks holiday every year.

"Hang on a minute," I said. "When they reach 55 they will have 26 weeks away."

"Plus statutory holidays," chipped in my personnel manager. "And there will be four weeks paid grandparents leave, to be taken within 12 months of the birth of each grandchild."

Into my nightmare nudged the smiling face of Bob who runs our Bedminster branch. Bob will be on a beano I thought. His seven fertile children presented him with five grandchildren in the past 12 months. He will never have to work again.

With so much bad news, I knew my finance director would soon disturb my sleep. "I have costed all the changes," he said, showing no emotion. "Some £3m in a full year. We will have to cut staff levels by 24 per cent to make budgeted profit."

The sales director looked agitated. "How can I cut staff levels with all my people on training courses or paternity leave?" I looked towards Tony Blair for guidance, but he had gone. Taking his place was a woman dressed in red, wearing a politically correct yellow ribbon. "Chair," she said, "can we turn to health and safety issues? The company must examine all its obligations in detail at every board meeting."

"Who are you?" I asked. "I'm your new enforcer, every company must have one," she said. "I assume everyone has read the latest directive, so I'd like the answers to a few questions."

"Does every new employee receive a copy of the 650-page guide to basic safety? Do all employees attend a health and safety meeting every week? Are employees qualified in first aid within three months of joining?" "But," I limply interrupted, "Half of them are at home looking after babies."

"If they are away from work for over three weeks, they must attend a refresher course before going back into the workplace."

"Who do you expect to run all these courses?" I asked. "That's obvious," she replied. "By law you must have a full-time health and safety officer for every ten employees. They will inspect each place of work every six months with the chief executive – that means you."

I started to ask how she thought I would have time to run the business, when she turned into a man. "I'm Bernard Lamar," he said. "From the European Directive Protective Agency. I'm here to check your company is ecologically compliant."

"My officers tell me you have failed to fulfil your environmental duties. We can fine you up to €100,000 for each offence but I will give you four weeks to become compliant."

"Where have we gone wrong?" I asked. "You fell down on 29 points: – You have not completed the weekly form showing the total use of packaging in your business. – You are not issuing a leaflet to every customer with a guide on how to recycle your packaging. – You have not produced a company strategy which aims to restrict waste to one wheelie bin per 100 employees. – Only ten per cent of your staff have attended a Euro Eco Course..."

I woke up covered in sweat. Alex called the doctor. "Pneumonia," was the diagnosis. I lay awake thinking about rules, regulations and European directives. We need fewer rules, but an army of bureaucrats produces more every year. Eventually they'll strangle the business world. I resolved to search for a place that runs on the minimum of rules, but I was grounded. Alex cut me off from the outside world and cancelled all appointments. Five days later, I was allowed downstairs and saw a notice the children had put on the kitchen wall.

Rule 1 – Alex makes all the decisions.
Rule 2 – If you think there is a need for a second rule, refer to rule 1.
Minimum rules, maximum efficiency. Absolute heaven.

25

Brainstorm in a teacup

We just had a directors' meeting with a difference. I decided to change our normal agenda and proposed a discussion on the future. Martin, our FD, suggested we should debate "risk assessment." I'm an optimist, so instead I asked everyone to suggest a new direction for future growth. I hoped this "directors' think tank" would tell us what we should do next.

We abandoned the boardroom and met in a pub. We had a private room for confidentiality and, most important, four bottles of wine to encourage free thinking. Our non-executive director, Patrick, offered a day at the Varsity match as a prize for the director with the best suggestion. We nominated him to judge the suggestions.

Mike, the property director, went first. "We are in the 'while you wait' service business," he said, "and have missed the best opportunity for decades – tattooing and body piercing." Eh? Nobody could see the logic behind Mike's idea. He dismissed the protests that tattooing didn't appeal to our market segment. "Think of the property gain," he said. "We would only need secondary sites and with a decent back room to do the work, showrooms can be less than 200 sq ft." Martin was turning white thinking about the product liability ear piercing could mean, so we moved swiftly on to James' suggestion.

"A telephone answering service," was James' idea. "There are call centres everywhere," interrupted Martin. "No, not a call centre," said James. "A proper telephone answering service for people like Access, Dixons and Alliance & Leicester who keep people waiting for 15 minutes listening to Handel's greatest hits, only to tell you they can't say anything due to the Data Protection Act. If those companies could claim that a real person answers calls within two rings, customers would flock to them." "That's not a business idea James," I objected. "It's the cry of a frustrated consumer. Let's have another suggestion."

"We ought to make an acquisition." Not surprisingly this idea came from the company lawyer. "We haven't made one for six years," he said wistfully. "Good point," interrupted Martin, licking his lips at the thought of weeks of due diligence. "Have you thought of who we should acquire?" I asked. "I was hoping to have some concrete suggestions for today's meeting," said Martin. "But I've been too busy with the year-end accounts."

I turned to Kit, our deputy chairman, whose clear thinking has often helped us through difficult discussions. He suggested a Christmas-shopping consultancy. "A personal service for busy executives. We could test the market through our London shops." "I don't think we'll bother," I said impatiently, keen to tell them about my suggestion. I was so confident I had a winner, I had already pencilled the Varsity match in my diary.

It was the "no-win no-fee" boys who gave me my business idea: a new chain of shops called Alright Jack, providing a comprehensive service to ensure every worker gets their legal entitlement. In addition to an accident-at-work counter, I will develop the Society for Sickness Entitlement, which will encourage every able-bodied employee to take his or her full quota of "sickies."

I expect to do particularly well with my free trial tribunal service. If you have the slightest hint of unfair dismissal, or even no hint at all, I will take up your case for £100 deposit. If I cannot get at least £1,000 in an out-of-court settlement you get your money back.

We would provide private investigators who use leer-sensitive cameras and grope-reactive dust to produce concrete evidence of inappropriate executive behaviour. We would provide experts well versed in the rules regarding harassment, paternity leave and health and safety. Our counselling service could advise disenchanted employees how to take time off due to stress and sound convincing. Our aim is to do so well that one in five customers can afford to give up work.

"So that's my idea, a chain of shops providing everything for the disloyal employee." After a stunned silence Kit found the snag. "Alright Jack will have trouble with its own employees. They will always be taking the company to court."

As we drifted to the bar, I saw Patrick in deep conversation with Martin. When they finished, Patrick came over with a sheepish grin on his face. "An entertaining afternoon, but the ideas were a complete disaster, so I am awarding the prize to Martin who is about to reveal record results. We don't need new ideas. We should stick to what we do well."

I was faced with a serious gap in my diary. "If I paid you the price of the tickets would you change your mind?" I pleaded.

The next time I saw Patrick was at the Varsity match.

26

Perfect your personnel

A few weeks ago, I played golf with my friend Gordon. We try and play once a month, setting off at 7.15am and finishing just after 10.00am, so I can get to the office for a full day's work.

Gordon usually wins. He sold his business a couple of years ago and now concentrates on "property interests." He is obviously doing pretty well: when he is not playing golf in Cheshire, he is playing at La Manga.

He doesn't talk much about his business – except to gloat about having a company with no employees. At a critical point in the match, he paused on the tee to offer advice: "I don't envy all the worries with 1,000 people working for you – you must be mad!" The comment was perfectly timed – I lost again.

With his smug remarks still ringing in my ears, I drove to the office only to be greeted by a succession of people problems. A sick leave epidemic had broken out in the Midlands. A solicitor was pursuing a claim for sexual harassment on behalf of a girl from Grimsby. Even more galling, our solicitor had suggested we settle a claim for £3,500. The claimant ran one of our worst-performing shops and almost certainly pinched at least £100 per week from the till!

It got worse. On my desk was a report from George, our personnel controller. It listed issues we are likely to face over the next few months – the working hours directive, racial discrimination, tighter redundancy rules, the likelihood of staff claiming compensation for stress at work.

George's list was so long, I thought he was winding me up. His catalogue of woe – from parental leave to sickness pay entitlement, not forgetting holiday pay, industrial injury, union recognition and disability benefit – could have earned him an oral warning for causing stress to his chairman.

The report would have had me on my hands and knees begging for mercy if it hadn't been for Jack Hammer.

Jack joined the company in May to work in our Northwich branch. He has never given us any hassle. No days off sick, no problems working Sundays. And I happen to know there is no prospect of him ever asking for paternity leave. He's great for sales, too. So who is this perfect employee?

Jack is a nodding cobbler who sits at the front of our shops, knocking in a nail and attracting customers. He never complains. And he works for free. Even better, Jack can be cloned. I now have 30 identical perfect employees around the country (another 40 will be delivered next month) – all totally untouched by legislation from Westminster or Brussels.

In January we will be holding a special millennium lunch and are currently seeking nominations for our millennium awards – Best Shoe Repairer, Best Manager, Best Key-Cutter. I was going to nominate Jack Hammer when I realised his limitations.

Jack just doesn't compare with John Wheelan in our Victoria branch who can serve three customers at once, have a conversation with each of them and still smile at the fourth person who is waiting to be served.

Jack wouldn't command the respect that John Quantrill gets running our warehouse. And he is nowhere near as good as Peter in Reading who brings a real buzz to our shop, enthuses customers – and puts loads of money in the till.

What bugs me about all this employment legislation is that when we pay out compensation, it usually goes to the people who least deserve it. Selfish, poor performers who have never made a real contribution to the company.

On reflection, George didn't deserve an oral warning because his report stung me into action. I took a careful look at each case where we have fallen foul of employment law. I now realise we have only ourselves to blame.

Consider the facts. Everyone who has taken us to a tribunal was employed following a job interview. Fifty per cent of claims come from someone who was promoted beyond their ability. Most industrial tribunals are the result of management not following procedure. Why? Because we did not train them properly.

It is time to stop whinging. Let's just accept these rules and turn them to our advantage. I know what I have to do: improve recruitment and management training and promote carefully.

And another thing, I am going to resist settling out of court. No more caving in before a tribunal to save money. Even if I am swelling the coffers of the legal profession, I have principles to stand by. And I must protect the interests of the majority of my employees who are a damned sight better than Jack Hammer, my nodding cobbler.

By the time I played my next game of golf with Gordon, I had come to terms with our personnel problems. Gordon's attitude seemed to be changing, too. His property business has been so successful he has opened an office and employed a secretary, a receptionist and an admin assistant.

I won the game – with ease.

27

The soft touch

"I can't imagine why you are tired," said Alex as I wearily sank into my chair. "Another easy day at the office with loads of people to help." Before I could reply she turned to watch Brookside with a "do not disturb" look on her face.

It's not just wives who don't realise what businessmen do to earn their living. Doctors and civil servants think we sit behind a desk shouting orders down the telephone. Once, I discussed management problems with a headmaster. "It's alright for you," he said. "You can fire people." To the outside world, chief executives are fat cats and ruthless vultures, smoking cigars, giving orders and firing every fourth employee.

Many other people are out of touch. Three years ago, I met a merchant banker who told me how he ran a business. "I put in a professional manager," he said. "If that doesn't work, I find another one." Just after he appointed his fourth chief executive, he himself was fired and the business went into receivership.

Serial sackings are a common feature of companies in trouble. The Sears' subsidiary, British Shoe Corporation, which dominated shoe retailing for 25 years, went through five chief executives in quick succession. The first handed over a 25 per cent market share, the last sold the seven per cent that remained.

There is a three-year cycle in this management merry-go-round. In year one, the honeymoon, the new broom sweeps away the past (good and bad), recruits new talent and launches a cost-cutting campaign. In year two, the hangover, when sales fall well below budget, he starts spending money to back up business. Things get worse rather than better, so in year three, the hanging, he is replaced with a new whizz-kid who starts the cycle over again.

History shows that you seldom make money by firing managers. And you don't solve fundamental problems by cutting costs. When a downturn comes (and it seems one is coming) ask, "Is it me or is it the market?" "Is the problem management, or the business I am in?"

When demand dies, it takes courage to stand up to an accountant who wants some ritual bloodletting to appease the bank. Nordstrom, the respected US retailer, gives this clue to its success: "During troubled times, we didn't get flustered. Fearful retailers got rid of people and slashed expenses while we invested in the future."

The adverts announced Brookside was over. Alex spoke: "What are you thinking about? Key-cutting I suppose."

"I was thinking you can still be nice and run a business."

"But when I rifled through your briefcase," confessed Alex, "I saw the staff changes, you fire people every week."

"We only fire people who shoot themselves in the foot," I said pompously. "Most leave due to poor timekeeping, or gross misconduct. I don't respect companies that dismiss staff who have done nothing wrong. It's not their fault they were in the wrong job."

"Are you so clever at picking people that you never have to dismiss or demote them?"

"You know that's not true," I replied. "Remember those sleepless nights worrying whether I should demote George and building myself into a frenzy before we fired that dreadful Dave?"

The decisions are seldom tough – the hard part is implementation. In the seventies I employed a buyer who was so bad, the business was at risk. She lacked fashion flair but possessed a talent for finding suppliers who ripped us off. The result was low margins, low sales and high mark-downs. You didn't have to issue written warnings in 1972 but it still took me six weeks to grasp the nettle. I waited for the problem to solve itself – hoping she would discover some charisma or even hand in her notice. The problem didn't disappear, she had to go. I rehearsed the meeting meticulously but when I suggested she could be far happier elsewhere, she burst into tears. Tact has never been my strongest suit.

Since then I have been thankful for people in personnel who take pride in a fair dismissal. For years I relied on Geoff who turned sacking people into an art form. He helped me implement lots of tough decisions – all good for the business and often good for the employee. Within a week you wonder what all the worrying was about.

I haven't lost much sleep recently, because we promote our own people. I learned my lesson when I imported a "superstar", thinking he would solve all our problems. It didn't work out and I haven't been tempted since. I promote to fill every vacancy. I know their strengths; they know our culture. If we pick the wrong person, they can have their old job back. It means a drop in salary but we make a one-off payment to compensate.

Alex rose from her chair. "You care for your employees more than your family," she said. "Why are you so nice to them?" I answered at once: "They are the people who look after our customers."

28

What's in a name?

What on earth does a "head of change and human energy" do?

I was just leaving for work, when a business card dropped out of my pocket. Alex swooped to pick it up. "You should get these reprinted," she said.

"What do you mean?" I asked.

"This says you are chairman and chief executive," she said, eyeing the sports bag over my shoulder. "You are semi-retired. What is it today? Tennis, golf, squash? In case you had forgotten, I am in London for the next two days, so you can play golf, tennis and snooker to your heart's content. Just make sure you leave the house tidy for Sheila."

Sheila is the lady who comes to tidy the house.

I rushed off for an early start at the office, so I could play tennis at 3.30pm. "Geoff wants to see you," said Barbara as I walked through the door. "He has been on a two-day seminar." Geoff got straight to the point. "I want to change my job title, I was totally out of place at the conference, I was the only personnel manager, everyone else was in human resources."

I can't see anything wrong with the title personnel. Most people can't spell it, but they know what the department does. It deals with people problems. At the slightest hint of an industrial tribunal, we call in personnel.

I told George I would think about his proposition, and decided to check what other companies did. On the way home, I bought all the quality newspapers and, after spending an hour tidying up for Sheila, sat down to study the situations vacant.

George had a point. There were many more human resources posts than personnel. And many that were even more innovative: people solutions manager, equal opportunities advocate, organisation development consultant and my favourite, head of change and human energy. But what struck me most were the job descriptions. A fast-growing B2B specialist promised the successful candidate would "work alongside our most senior managers, and identify strategies to improve leadership." A company that claimed to be a "rising star in the delivery of time sensitive information on a global stage," was looking for candidates to "put in place systems for reporting progress against the key deliverables, ensuring resources are mobilised to best effect." A number one provider of systems solutions wanted a professional to "create and drive HR strategies that would critically lead a programme of change within the long-term business planning process." I got the feeling human resources people think they run the business. A bit like finance directors.

Things got worse as I thumbed through the appointments pages. Some organisations, particularly new government departments, were not just advertising for one HR executive, they wanted a full set of them. They bragged about the size of their organisation. "The dimensions of our HR department are massive," said one. "The department has trail-blazing dynamics. You will have a substantial multi-site staff resource," claimed another. "The demanding senior post has vast organisational scale, cultural and structural change and the opportunity to be at the cutting edge of reform," said an advert by the new Department for Work and Pensions. A quick glance at the public appointment pages proves that countless quangos are still being created.

A friend of mine recently pointed out an odd fact. "Many personnel departments have the highest labour turnover in the business. You should never expect the head of HR to be particularly good at picking people." So what should you expect of them? One leader in global communication was looking for the following superstars: "a dynamic individual with entrepreneurial spirit who challenges the status quo"; "a real team player leading from the front with intuition and vision"; "a well-networked doer and deliverer, with a strong strategic mind and pragmatic hands-on style"; "a born leader and proactive professional with excellent interpersonal skills, and real persuading presence." Put these people together in their new dynamic HR department, and you have the recipe for complete disaster, an explosion of pompous people challenging each other's status quo. Any business with a big HR team will find it easy to cut costs when the recession really arrives.

I tidied up carefully for Sheila the following morning, and as soon as I got to the office, the expectant face of George popped round the door. I stood my ground. "We are not ready for human resources at Timpson, George," I started firmly. "You are a great personnel manager and that's what I want to call you." To emphasise the point, I arranged a smart new sign for his office door (and made a modest adjustment to his salary).

When Alex arrived home, she saw a pile of sports clothing lying by the washing machine. "I had lunch with Judy while I was in London, her husband Jack's retired, and guess what? He does the washing in their house now." I stopped her in her tracks when I produced a new business card. "Look, I've got a new job title, I won't have time for washing. I'm not just chairman, I am also head of care and common sense, I won't be semi-retired for some time."

29

Businessman seeks explanation

I don't think I'm particularly sensitive, but I was very upset the other day when a banker asked me, "Don't you think it's time you brought in some professional management?"

For 15 years nearly all our major appointments have been internal. Home-grown succession has been good for our business. But the banker's remark bothered me. Perhaps we do miss out by excluding the wider world of management expertise. To learn more, I studied one broadsheet's recruitment pages. It told me all I needed to know about professional managers.

First observation: why do modern executives have to hide behind obscure titles such as "head of contact excellence" when most companies would call them the sales manager. If they can create new titles, so can I. The personnel manager who approved this advert should be renamed "head of gobbledegook." Sadly, we don't know who they are because their business hides behind a pompous and anonymous description – "leading global leisure player with diversified portfolio."

It's interesting to read why there is a vacancy. *"Rapid growth in product portfolio and development in customer contact methodologies demands a top-notch individual reporting to director of contact centre operations to drive customer contact management and deliver enhanced operational and service standards across five sites."* In truth, the company probably has a major sales problem and hopes to find a superstar to bring them back on track.

The sort of person who gets this job won't expect to do it on their own; they want someone who will *"Define, implement and monitor world-class service delivery standards at all points of interaction."* The successful candidate will expect a couple of assistants and use outside consultants to fulfil such an ambitious task.

The simplest part of the job is: *"To develop and roll out conversion strategies of individual customer segments which maximise the sales."* That means producing a sales plan. More dangerous is the requirement to: *"Benchmark contact handling capabilities and customer delivery internally and externally."* As soon as someone mentions "benchmarking," it won't be long before they talk about market research and focus groups. This new executive will spend a lot of the company's money.

But they won't be spending it on their own because they are also required to: *"Ensure best-in-class practice is shared across contact centres through creation and management of Excellence Environments."* This will mean gathering as many people as possible for a three-day seminar in the business centre of their local Holiday Inn. Whole sections of the management team will doze through the day in a hot conference room before being released to the bar to get pissed at the company's expense and slag off the senior management.

If you're thinking of applying for this job, check the section that describes the ideal candidate. Don't be put off by *"Graduate Calibre"* –

you don't need a degree, just look intelligent at the interview. Don't worry about being a *"senior management contact centre professional"*; that simply means sales person. As does *"a recognised sales/service guru with hands-on experience at contact centre and contact monitoring technology."* But in order to offer *"diverse blue chip B2C experience,"* you will need to be a serial job-hunter.

To provide *"demonstrable success in developing benchmark processes and competency models, expertise in devising and managing learning and development solutions,"* you must be good at company politics. To be a *"strategic thinker with commercial, action-orientated approach and a natural leader, motivator and coach with the ability to challenge perceptions and build strong relationships across multi-site environment,"* you should be pompous and self-opinionated. So there you have it, a detailed description of a professional manager. An intelligent-looking arrogant sales person who plays company politics while building an empire and spending lots of money before flitting off to another job.

After much careful consideration, I have decided to reject the banker's advice and keep the company running with our present bunch of amateurs.

irritations

There is just a danger that a columnist who is regularly irritated by the world around him can – no matter how entertainingly – degenerate into sounding like a grumpy old man. The things that get to John, however, are sometimes familiar (mobile phones on trains) but just as often revealing and important (the onset of stress, the bullying tactics of big companies). Prepare to be surprised.

30

The jargon game

A young banker recently introduced me to a game that relieves boredom on the motorway – it's called "beards." Before overtaking, select a car you think is driven by a beard. Score ten points if you are correct, lose a point if your choice is clean-shaven. My personal best between London and Manchester is 68 points. My secret is to pick Volvos.

I've invented a Virgin Rail version, called "mobile phone." You have to find the carriage champion. Award fellow passengers a point for making a call and two for receiving one. Between Euston and Crewe the winner usually scores over 20 points.

A recent trip to Liverpool produced a great example. On the way to

Milton Keynes a close contest developed between a prematurely bald guy, who answered the telephone with a very sharp "Wilkins", and a powerfully dressed woman in blue who was desperate not to be over-heard. She spoke so softly that she had to repeat herself. We heard everything twice.

The bald tycoon was doing a deal. "Hi JP, just been at the sharp end – we need more number crunching before D-Day..."

The lady in blue answered her phone with a precise "Penny Parker" – she was on the defensive. "God Peter, it was a nightmare, they're absolutely paranoid about negative sentiment...."

The tycoon tapped his laptop between calls, clicking his teeth with excitement. "JP, let me explain. Done a sensitivity and can't see a problem with double-digit projection – all pretty robust."

Penny shot into the lead when she received two calls in quick succession. "They're moving all the deck chairs Malcolm... Yes, big-hitting Simon... marked my card for a roll out of outsourcing and downsizing. He's playing hard ball, but finance is ring-fenced."

Back came Wilkins. "It's coming up in spades. I've thrown a lot of numbers around our ball park to see how they fall. It flies at any level – bound to wash its face..."

Before reaching Stafford, Mr Bald caught up with Penny when he gave JP another call. "Can't say much more on the train, but let's be proactive. I vote we give Jim a good lick of the spoon if he delivers in our time frame."

As we approached Crewe, it looked like a dead heat until Penny received the winning call. "Yes Pete, serious is not the word. We'll never get the clearance for project Polar Bear now. They've closed the stable door and scored a monumental own goal..."

Wilkins 20 points, Penny Parker 22.

Back in my car, I was happy to be free of business speak. I switched on the radio. "City fans were well made up early doors when the boy Kennedy came good – played phenomenal with a left foot not a million miles from your Beckhams. Top drawer." Sadly, I understood every word.

So why don't people use plain English? Well, because jargon works – as I discovered at the office the following day. I was trying to promote my latest idea of selling walking sticks in our shops, but there was considerable opposition. "With respect John, we don't want to lose the plot," pleaded George. "Walking sticks hardly fit our core market."

I decided to use a favourite trick. To put on the charm, keep using the words "exactly" and "absolutely."

"Absolutely, I see exactly where you're coming from. It's not normally my style, but let's for once turn things on their head – no telling where it could send us..."

"You mean a bit of lateral thinking."

"Exactly. Got it in one. Keep an open mind. Trial them in 20 shops and come to me if it stacks up." The words worked and so did the walking sticks, which George now claims were his idea.

Flushed with success, I decided to use the technique when I got home on Friday. There was a tricky problem that weekend. We were going to my brother-in-law's birthday party in Hertfordshire; by chance, Manchester City were playing in Luton.

I had a plan. If my wife Alex would spend the afternoon with an old school chum near Dunstable, I could look at the new site, go to the football match and still be in good time for the party. Perfect. But this wasn't Alex's idea.

"I've got a game plan for the weekend," I shouted through the front door. "How about seeing Maggie at Dunstable for a few hours, I've plenty to do."

"I suppose you think you are going to watch the football."

"Exactly, just an idea, thought I'd run it up the flagpole – see if you'd salute it." She didn't salute it – I had scored an own goal – it all went pear-shaped, big time.

31

The dog ate my diary

I couldn't help hearing the telephone conversation next door. "What's got into him today?" It was Barbara, my secretary, speaking to Alex my wife. "He's in a foul mood. I'm going to keep clear."

It was only 9.30 and I already knew this wasn't going to be a good day. My usual 40-minute journey to the office had taken over an hour. Although I set off in plenty of time, I met a new set of roadworks on the A49 and was nearly late for my 8.30 appointment. I was meeting a man who had telephoned me the week before. He wanted to demonstrate a revolutionary system of stock-taking, which he said was not to be missed. He had a tight schedule and we agreed to meet early in the morning. But I did miss the stock-taking revolution – he failed to turn up. I rang his mobile, and found him on the M4 travelling towards Maidenhead. "Sorry," he said. "It's in my personal organiser for next week."

Wondering what to with the extra hour now available, I looked at a computer printout lying on my desk. It showed detailed sales for April. It was a patchy performance. Not bad overall, but some shops had dragged us down.

I looked at one of the culprits. Why on earth had we dropped 15 per cent in Swindon? I gave them a ring and got straight through to Dean, the manager.

"It's the car parking," he said. "The whole town is up in arms, they're redeveloping the old multi-storey so there are fewer spaces. And they've shoved up the charges."

On the next page I spotted an even worse performance in Cardiff. I dialled their number. "Everything came to a grinding halt for the International," said Gwyn. "Wales won, but we lost."

Everyone I spoke to had a good excuse. The road system had been changed in Southampton. A new competitor was advertising ridiculously low prices in Winchester and Tesco had moved in at Workington.

I was about to investigate a horrible result in Hawick when Alex phoned. "Problems with the plumber," she said. "He was an hour late so I gave him a ring. He said he can't make it today. A bout of sickness. Short staffed. I don't think he listens to women. Oh, and by the way, don't forget we are going out tonight, we need to set off no later than 6.15."

I rang the plumber. "I hear you can't do the job at my house – can you recommend another plumber?"

"I'll give you priority and send someone straight away," he replied.

Barbara brought in my post bag and on top of the pile was a customer complaint. A lady from Fulham had called at our shop at 5.15 on Friday to find it was shut. She had to make a special journey the following day to rescue the tankard we had engraved for the best man at her son's wedding. By chance, the area manager was in the office that morning so I asked him to come and see me. "First thing I've heard about it," he said. "Mind you, Friday was my day off and the shop was being run by a relief manager. We've recently had a lot of sickness and holidays and I haven't got the staff to cover."

I had a meeting at 2.30 to discuss stock levels, late delivery and just-in-time management. The meeting was due to start when Barbara popped into the office. "You won't believe this, but the meeting is delayed until three o'clock. George is stuck in traffic and Phillip has a visitor who is running late." It was 3.15 before we started talking about prompt deliveries and it was well after five when we finished.

After everybody had left the office, my eyes went back to the computer printout – I was still worried about the poor performers and decided to try one more shop. Bill in Grimsby had been trading badly since Christmas. I've known Bill for years and this is the first time I can remember him producing a poor performance. "To be honest," said Bill, "I've not been on top form for some time. Nothing to do with the shop. I've split up with my partner, my mum's very ill and I've got money problems."

I listened to Bill for some time. He'd certainly hit a sticky patch. It was hardly surprising that the shop turnover had suffered. I asked him to set out all his problems in a note so I could consider a company loan and promised to make sure his area manager called the following day.

Bill's honest reply was a refreshing change to the barrage of excuses I had been hearing all day – he restored my faith in human nature.

By the time I had rearranged the paper on my desk into neater piles and put some possible weekend work into my briefcase, it was 5.45.

My trip home was better than the morning. The roadworks had almost disappeared and the journey only took 40 minutes. When I walked through the door at 6.25, Alex was pacing up and down ready to go out. "Sorry," I said, "stuck in traffic, road works on the A49."

32

True Lies

"I've got a busy day tomorrow," said Alex as she turned over to go to sleep. "Can I have my tea at quarter to seven?"

"Sorry," I replied. "I'm visiting shops in south Wales and have to be off at 5.45am."

"You're too old for these early starts. Can't you work ordinary hours like everyone else?"

"I have to beat the M6 traffic. If I leave it too late, I'll be stuck in Birmingham."

I lingered shaving and couldn't find my car keys, so it was 6am before I set off.

In Middlewich, just before the motorway, I stopped for petrol, a paper and breakfast. (Don't tell Alex, but I like Eccles cakes at 6.15am.) The Shell garage was severely short of stock – no pork pies, no Eccles cakes and the only sandwiches left were cheese and pickle. Yuck. "Want a receipt?" said the bored cashier as I handed over my credit card. I nodded. "Short of stock?" I asked. "The manager failed to order," she said. "Can you imagine it, the hottest week of the year and no drinks or ice creams. Bad management, that's what it is, bad management."

I knew I was too late even before I got to Birmingham. The trafficmaster gizmo in my car showed the delays had already begun. The telephone rang. It was my son James. "Where are you?" he said.

"Just approaching Birmingham, about to be stuck in a queue. Where are you?"

"On the A34 by Oxford, I'll be in Newbury before eight. I set off at 5.15am, you should have done the same."

I came to a grinding halt just by Hilton Park services and listened to the news for the third time that morning. "Everyone knows," said a government minister, "that if we keep building more roads, we will create extra traffic, and put more pollution in the environment." I've never understood that argument. There I was, surrounded by cars and lorries going nowhere, with their engines polluting the atmosphere. Inside the vehicles were people being paid lots of money to sit still and do nothing. It's bad management, I thought. Bad management by the government. All this "everyone knows that new roads make things worse" is just an excuse to cover up their inefficiency.

Another item came on the news. "It's a well-known fact," said a spokesman, "that if we fail to join the euro, Britain will face a long period of economic decline." I'm out of tune with that one as well. I studied economics at university and have the "BA" after my name to prove that economics is an art, not a science. Economists have two things in common with accountants: they are both experts on the past, but can't predict the future any better than long-range weather forecasters. No-one knows whether the euro will be of economic benefit; it's a political decision. I like my politics to be home-grown. I don't fancy being part of the United States of Europe. But politics seems to be about turning unsubstantiated theories into reality by using phrases such as "it's a well-known fact," "everyone knows" and, of course, "of course."

Every time you listen to the radio, you are bombarded with a load of well-known facts that aren't true. You're also told that "everyone agrees" with things that you totally disagree with.

The next news item was about paternity leave and flexible working hours. I thought these were fine in principle until I realised who was going to carry the cost. We are getting to the stage where government makes businesses organise and pay for everything; they get the credit while we get the blame – and the bill.

I switched from Radio 5 to *The Today Programme* on Radio 4. Flexible working seemed to be the topic of the day. "Anyone who doesn't understand the advantages that will stem from flexible working hours," said the spokesman, "is totally out of tune with modern thinking." I guess that's me, I thought. Perhaps Alex is right, I am getting too old for this game. After all, I was one of those "Luddites" who, when the e-commerce craze came along, bravely said that the dot-com bonanza would end in tears.

After 45 minutes, the traffic started to move gently towards Walsall and the RAC building. I'd quite enjoyed the stop on the motorway; it gave me a welcome chance to think. I almost resented the traffic moving again. It meant I was back to work.

Before I reached the M5, the telephone rang. It was George, one of our area managers. "I want to change the prices in Southend," he said. "There's a guy on the market who is cutting keys at a £1 a time."

"Leave your prices where they are," I said. "It's a well-known fact that cutting prices doesn't increase turnover. All you will do is store up trouble." I thought everyone agreed with that.

33

Under pressure

A few weeks ago I was looking forward to a day full of meetings, but the woman due at 10am never arrived (she said there was nothing in her diary). The man expected at 4pm rang with an agitated apology, claiming that his wife's mother was seriously ill. No-one seems able to cope with the pressure of heavy workloads anymore.

In my spare time I visited a friend who was recovering from a heart bypass. When it comes to hospital visiting I stare around the ward at other patients and talk nervously, mostly about myself. I thought my friend would be interested in my busy week, lots of travelling punctuated by games of golf and tennis. "You make me feel tired," he said. "I wish I had a third of your energy. How do you fit everything in?"

"We've been invited out next Tuesday," said Alex that night during the Coronation Street commercial break. "Sorry," I said. "I'm afraid I'm at a conference in London, followed by golf at Hankley Common."

"It's alright for the semi-retired," said Alex. "Rushing round the country with your golf clubs, acting half your age. I just hope your life insurance is up-to-date."

The truth is that I love being busy and was looking forward to the non-stop action of a full diary. The next morning I took my son Henry to the school bus before setting off for the office. I was thinking about a watch repair meeting when I suddenly realised my mistake – I should have been playing tennis with Tom. I'd forgotton. Five years ago such a blunder would have seriously bothered me. Any stupid error of this nature would have triggered stress that would only be eased after a doctor gave me some happy pills. But I was so relaxed when I turned up – late – for my match with Tom, that I played my best tennis for months. More evidence I thought that I had finally learned to cope with stress.

Then I had a bad day at the office. We were gazumped on a deal I had worked on for months. Then I missed the watch repair meeting – I had put the wrong date in my diary. Even so, I stayed calm until, on the way home, I filled my car up with unleaded petrol. My car takes diesel. Two hours later, the car was towed away and I got the first hint of depression. A twinge that announces oncoming misery like the first sign of flu.

When I woke the following morning, I dreaded facing the busy day ahead. I could not get that petrol pump out of my mind. Suddenly, our business that had looked so full of promise was beset with problems. I turned them over and over in my mind but couldn't come to any conclusions. I normally enjoy chatting in the office but that day other people were just a pain. I tried to look interested but couldn't fool Barbara. "Are you alright?" she said.

"I've just got a lot on my mind. Could you cancel my meetings in London on Thursday? Tell them it's pressure of work."

Alex was waiting when I got home. "I've been speaking to Barbara," she said. "She says you are bad-tempered. It's your fault, you do far too much. Conferences in London, golf goodness-knows-where and then you leave early to play tennis. Who do you think you are? You are nearly 60. You know where to go to get help."

Next morning I went to the doctor. The receptionist greeted me cheerfully. "You look well," she said. I tried to smile, realising that my depressed state was well camouflaged by a healthy golf-course tan. I waited for half an hour looking at obscure magazines, not reading a word. The waiting room, as always, was full of ashen-faced people. I wondered whether I should face this depression on my own and not waste the doctor's time.

Exchanging my prescription for a packet of happy pills at the pharmacy made me feel a whole lot better. But I was still miserable the following morning and dreaded yet another day surrounded by superbly competent colleagues whose decisiveness would put me to shame. Just thinking about them made me tired.

I heeded Alex's advice and took the day off. I planned to do nothing at all but sit in front of the television. "You must do something," said Alex. "You can't mope around the house all day." She was right; staring into space would just make things worse; so I decided to write this article. I usually write about more light-hearted subjects, but stress is a serious subject that can affect us all. I'm no exception.

It took me 90 minutes to dictate the first draft; then I discovered that the tape machine wasn't working. But I didn't panic, I just started over. I guess you've just got to try and keep things in perspective. But it's not easy, I know.

If you don't get depressed, lucky you. I am jealous. If you suffer like me, then I hope it helps to know that other people suffer, too. If nothing else, this article might help me remember not to fill my diesel car with unleaded petrol.

34

Act your age, not your shoe size

I don't think I'm old fashioned, but I keep meeting modern business improvements that make matters worse.

A few weeks ago I played snooker with a friend whose business has supplied supermarkets for years. "You won't believe what's happened," he said. "Three months ago they (a well-known supermarket) appointed a 22-year-old buyer for my product area. Last week he de-listed one of my main lines. He didn't even speak to me. I got an e-mail instructing me to discontinue deliveries immediately. My warehouse is full of the stuff all packaged and ready to go." He missed an easy red before continuing. "I was so upset I rang his supervisor, who I have known for years. Two days later I got another e-mail. The 22-year-old de-listed four more lines at a potential cost to me of £350,000. I rang him in desperation. 'That's what happens,' he said, 'if you go over my head'."

Abuse of corporate power is nothing new. I was travelling to a shoe fair in Milan 25 years ago with a footwear supplier from Bacup, when the air stewardess came and asked him for £15. "What for?" he asked. "Champagne for your friends at the front of the plane," she said. They weren't his friends, they were buyers from the British Shoe Corporation taking advantage of their 25 per cent market share.

Two weeks later my travel companion rang me up. "I have a problem," he said. "BSC says that if I continue to supply shoes to you, they won't place any more orders."

When a company resorts to blackmail it's best to blow it out into the open. So I wrote to BSC's buying director asking him to confirm the restriction in writing. He replied that there was no truth in the rumour.

Today's common tactic is a circular letter announcing a change in contract terms. Philip Green quickly told Arcadia suppliers he was reducing their prices. Recently a cut-price retailer unilaterally decided to take higher discounts for extended credit terms. The attitude is: "We will change the terms of our contract whether you like it or not."

One supermarket puts up a poster in the office reception, listing its ten worst suppliers. It's an interesting insight into the way the company treats people. Salesmen have plenty of time to study the poster, too, because the buyers are not only bullies, they also have bad manners. They keep salesmen waiting for up to two hours; if the buyer loses patience and leaves, the next month he could join the list of worst suppliers.

Why do they do it? Do these companies think it's a smart way to do business? They treat buying and selling as a battle of wits and think the toughest tactics will win. The attitude of the big buyer is, "you need me more than I need you." They forget that for every action there is a reaction. There might be a short-term price advantage, but the victim will try to get his own back. Quality suffers when loyalty to a buyer is based on fear. I saw what happened at BSC. Their bullying backfired and eventually Saxone, Freeman, Hardy and Willis, Trueform and Curtess disappeared from the high street.

When I was a shoe buyer in the seventies, I had to find ways to compete with BSC. In contrast to them, I was nice to my suppliers who, in return, gave me preferential treatment. Providing an excellent service to a competitor was one way suppliers could get their own back on the industry's bully.

My approach was thought wet, weak and old-fashioned, but it worked so well that we have tried to co-operate closely with suppliers ever since. We let them see all our figures, and issue an identity card so they can visit our shops and ask the staff questions. Any supplier can complain to me with a guarantee they won't be victimised by their buyer. To make sure we continue to uphold our standards, I am sending a copy of this article to all our suppliers. Good buying isn't just about getting the cheapest price.

Small and medium-sized companies have been pushed about and abused by the "big boys" for far too long. It's time to stop people who think bullying is good business. Perhaps the government should come to the rescue.

Please don't think we're a soft touch. I believe there is nothing wrong with being commercial. Bad suppliers deserve all they get, but good ones must be treated with respect. They should feel like partners, not adversaries. Too many buyers gain a short-term advantage by ruining a long-term relationship.

It's up to management to set the right moral tone. It's ethically wrong to allow buyers to take undue advantage of weak suppliers. Be warned, history has shown that an immoral culture can lead to bribery and corruption and I don't just mean expensive gifts at Christmas.

I argued above that government should introduce anti-business bullying legislation, but I hope it doesn't. For us, being old-fashioned and nice to suppliers has worked really well. If others copy the idea, we would lose a considerable competitive advantage.

Knee deep in fertiliser

I like holidays and never more so than last month's. I had suffered weeks of interference from the regulators – VAT inspectors, asbestos surveys, equal opportunity questionnaire, health & safety trying to shut our shop in Scarborough and a traffic warden who gave me a ticket in Nottingham. Mustique was never so inviting.

Ten minutes into my first tennis lesson with Richard, the pro, the rain started. When it stopped Richard asked me to check the court. "Is it slippery?" he said. "No," I said, realising I was paying for the lessons whether we played or not. "Just to make it clear," said Richard, "it's at your risk." Health & Safety had followed me on holiday.

After tennis I joined my friend, Chris, for a rum punch at Basil's Bar. "Don't talk to me about red tape," he said. "I've been surrounded by it for years." I ordered another rum punch and Chris told me about his business.

Chris has spent his life selling chicken manure. His father, with the help of a Dr Novokosky, developed a garden fertiliser that was six times more effective than ordinary manure when applied at the standard one pint per square yard. So he called it 6X.

This is no ordinary chicken shit. Neat droppings burn plants and kill them, but Chris's father discovered that the perfect mix of droppings and wood shavings can transform a garden.

You might think chicken shit was an area for regulators to avoid, but you'd be wrong. First problem: packaging.

The product was supplied in 33lb bags because this was the heaviest that Chris's mother could carry down the garden – Dad knew a lot of women gardeners and wanted to keep to a feminine load. This is still the size today, although Europe requires it to be labelled 15kg.

Chris's father advertised on the bag that the contents could cover 220sq yds of lawn. He recommended measuring with an empty half-pint processed pea tin – 440 measures were in every bag.

Such quaint but precise instructions were seen as a challenge by a trading standards inspector in Buckinghamshire, who could only fill his pea tin 432 times. Dad claimed that the weight loss was due to evaporation, but the man's lawn had been shortchanged by four square yards. Dad was prosecuted.

At the second attempt, the case succeeded. "When making such specific claims, you run a big risk," said the judge. "I suggest a vaguer measurement." Dad took the advice, abandoned the tin of peas and substituted "double handfuls."

Once he'd added advice about wearing gloves, made clear that the 15kg was "when packed", and added a warning to prevent dogs with a delicate digestive system from eating more than half a double handful, there was no more trouble with the packaging.

You may be relieved to know that the 6X does not come from battery hens – it is produced by broilers who have a short but just as miserable life (41 days) from birth to chicken nugget.

Legislation has tried to come to their rescue, too. Chickens used to be crowded into incredibly compact conditions. Now farmers are restricted to 25 kilos of full-grown birds per square metre. Good news for the chicken, but bad news for 6X. Chickens like huddling together and, despite the extra statutory space, still stay in a tight bunch – so the droppings are no longer evenly spread through the shavings. An extra mixing process has been added to the production.

Organic products vary according to nature, but everything today from bananas to beefburgers must be standardised – chicken manure is no exception. Right now, 6X waits with trepidation while a working party determines the definition of Euros**t.

Chris put a third rum punch in front of me and my mind wandered. Sensible rules can make things better, but there's always a danger that regulation will take over the world. Last month, one of our shop openings was delayed by two weeks because the building inspector was on leave. Another shop was closed while we waited for our landlord to find an electrician with the right credentials to change a fuse.

I estimate that 15 per cent of the British workforce are policemen, checking safety, approving plans, weighing and measuring. They have the power to stand in the way of progress. And they are growing in number. By 2005, one quarter of all workers could be regulating the rest of us. Soon, someone will see the need to regulate the regulators. Imagine, an outer band of red tape that checks on the checkers, making sure that no-one escapes the proper procedure. I hope this new superpower will tackle the most sinister side of the nanny state – bribery and corruption. Too often you suspect the easiest route to obtain approval is a wad of £20 notes passed to the official.

Remember, when giving power to the regulator, power can corrupt.

36

Trust Me

The past few weeks have tested the very values of my business philosophy. I have always believed the best way to do business is to trust people. Despite being thought a soft touch, it has worked. By giving trust you receive it in return. Trusted suppliers deliver on time and trusted shop staff look after your customers.

Three months ago, we purchased a competitor. The new business has gone well apart from the 20 new employees we caught pinching money from the till. Based on that experience, £2m of the £70m turnover could be going straight into employees' pockets.

With my faith in human nature shattered, I went home to seek sympathy from Alex.

"It's a scandal," she said before I could get through the door. "A woman I know in Winsford who is on disability benefit coaches the local girls' football team. She is as fit as a fiddle, but turns up for her annual medical in a wheelchair." Alex could see my mind was still in the office. "Don't worry about my news, what's happened at work? You say I never take an interest," she said. "Not true," I replied. "Remember your idea of giving everyone a birthday cake?" "Yes," she said, "did it go down well?" "Very well with the employees but not with the finance department who say the Revenue will call it benefit in kind and could impose penalties. The Revenue will sting us but seems happy to watch our competitors pay casual labour in cash and fiddle their VAT." "Never mind," said Alex, "at least tomorrow you will be getting away from the business". I was due to start two weeks' jury service. I had a large beer and went to bed hoping sleep would save me from the stress.

Within minutes I was queuing at the back door to heaven under a sign 'Abuse of Power Tribunal.' I had guilty thoughts about the birthday cakes and benefit in kind but needn't have worried, I was on the jury as Lord Justice Benefit of Doubt and Justice Common Sense tried a succession of rogue traders.

The first was a venture capitalist who picked up a £10m pay-off when one of his pet projects proved a disaster. "Please look at exhibit A," said John Scruples QC. "A job application that includes the following: 'I masterminded a major change in strategy and appointed a new management team with clear targets that increased budgeted profit by £40m over the previous year.' I don't challenge the correctness of this C.V. said Scruples, "but it distorts the truth. The defendant may have written a budget showing a £40m profit, but he managed to produce a £40m loss."

The venture capitalist was quickly replaced by a man who used to work in our local Planning Office. He gave permission for the development of an oriental duck farm, including a farm manager's cottage being extended to five bedrooms. When the duck farm was a financial disaster, the cottage fetched a six figure sum. The local Planning Officer now lives in a particularly posh part of Lancashire, but our learned friend Mr Scruples was unable to prove bribery or corruption.

A fashion buyer from the Midlands was next in the dock. This was a cut and dried case of corruption. For four years, five per cent of the sterling value of orders he placed in India was lodged in a Swiss bank account. He was sent down for 250 years, and replaced in front of the judge by a corporate lawyer accused of obtaining £1m through false pretences. "Putting it bluntly," said Scruples, "you charge £800 per hour to argue silly legal points at your clients' expense, including a day's discussion about what would happen if a meteor struck the head office building between exchange and completion." The lawyer was prepared to spend days arguing his case until Judge Common Sense ordered him to write a 10-year sentence without a verb or a comma.

He was replaced by a security officer, working for London Underground, who would not allow contractors on site without paying a minimum of £250. The judge was unimpressed that he needed the money to look after his children because his wife was in prison for several charges of shop lifting.

"What can you expect," said Mr P Correct QC, defending. "If you give individuals the burden of enforcing rules and applying regulations, you put them under tremendous pressure. They should be forgiven the occasional small bribe or tiny bit of corruption. It's the system's fault he appears before this court with a tarnished reputation."

A Health & Safety Officer from South Wales was taking the stand when Alex woke me up. "What's the problem?" she said, "you're covered in sweat and shouting who can I trust, who can I trust?" "Don't worry," I said, "it was only a dream."

But it was an odd sort of dream. I had already met all the defendants who appeared before the Court of Abuse Tribunal. This was no fantasy, they were real people demonstrating a real problem. "What's this about trust?" said Alex. "Are you changing your business philosophy?" "Don't worry," I said, " the only way to run a business is to trust people. Honesty is a great investment." "But how can you trust people?" continued Alex "if so many are on the fiddle?" "That's simple," I replied "you pick people very carefully. You only choose those you can trust." "Be careful," said the voice of 'P Correct QC' from my dream, "don't violate the human rights of people who can't be trusted."

Topical

It's to the credit of any columnist when, in making a compilation such as this, one does not have to include detailed footnotes to explain long-forgotten names and references that seemed so important at the time. Well, we still have to come to a decision about the euro but John's column about Timpson and the dot-com era brilliantly captures the mood of the bemused sceptic in that heady period.

37

Ideas that work

I woke up with mixed feelings on New Year's Day. Don't get me wrong. We'd had a fantastic party the night before – fancy dress, champagne, fireworks, Auld Lang Syne. But the next day, I suddenly felt much, much older.

If the millennium bug had struck, it wouldn't have been so bad. But it didn't. At midnight, the only cloud still hanging over the technological revolution disappeared. This signalled the all clear for a generation of teenage tycoons to develop e-commerce to their hearts' content. So we're faced with a *Sunday Times* rich list full of under-25-year-old nerds, with the Queen trailing in 75th place.

On January 1, 2000, I was finally confirmed as yesterday's man.

But now, two months later, I've come to terms with the technology. I'm becoming rather excited about all this dot-com business, and the more money we lose on our web site, the more enthusiastic I get. It's quite a transformation. Until now, I've been the ultimate cyber-luddite. My office bears no trace of a lap-top. I do have an e-mail address but, to make sure I get a reply, I've always thought it better to send a letter.

Our web site developed by chance. Every business has its technocrat who bashes his computer frantically out of office hours. We have Russ – our web master who until recently had been shackled as a shoe repairer. At first, I didn't understand what Russ was doing. He sat in front of his computer producing no obvious benefit to the business. He might as well have been playing Tomb Raider or Solitaire.

Then one day in June, he proudly presented the first few pages of our web site. It showed a map of our shops, pictures of the directors and a page where you could order our engraved house signs.

In August, Russ took his first e-mail order – a rustic sign for a house in Harpenden called "Windy Hollow." In September, he sold two more. In October, we sold a house sign every week. During November, he put more products on the web – pet discs, engraved tankards and keys cut by code number. In December, we sold 14 house signs, engraved a pet tag for a poodle in Auckland, New Zealand, and cut ten keys for a customer in California.

This was so encouraging I asked Russ to give me computer coaching. In just four hours, he had me surfing the web. I borrowed his lap-top over the weekend. By Saturday night, the novelty had worn off and I had my routine read of the Sunday financial press. It was full of e-commerce kids coming to the market at prodigious prices.

So I did some research to value our fledgling Timpson.com. I estimated the total market value of all UK internet stocks at £165bn. These companies make a combined loss of £1bn on a total turnover of £2.4bn. But, I am told, the current loss is irrelevant. All will be well within three years, when they will turn a profit of £40bn. My Sunday papers had tipped most internet stocks as a "buy."

I thought about these figures. For a profit of £40bn, you'd need sales of £800bn or £2,000 for every adult in the country. Within three years we'd be spending ten per cent of our hard-earned cash on the net. It might be possible. But is it feasible?

I consulted my daughter who embraced the technological age long ago and checks her e-mail every day. She went shopping on the web just before Christmas. She hadn't managed to find a costume for the millennium party. She'd searched for "fancy dress" and come up with a catalogue of bizarre rubber outfits - not exactly suitable for the occasion. She did manage to buy a book but it took ages: 24 minutes from switching on, to placing the order. Even if I can match her pace, it would take me 12.5 working days to spend my £2,000 share of the e-commerce cake.

I showed my analysis to Russ who told me I'd got it wrong. "Computers double their speed every two months," he said. "Far from being glued to the screen, the internet will save you time. You could even play more golf." I walked away convinced that, at the current rate of growth, our web site will be selling one million house signs a week by 2005.

Impressed with our success, we have started a second site, CityCobbler.com. It's a real world-beater. Contact us on the net and a motorbike will appear within minutes to collect your shoes. We'll lend you a pair of quality shoes for two hours while we make yours as good as new. Russ says the signs are already good, with two repairs in the first week and six in the second. He predicts we should reach 500,000 within three years.

Based on Russ's forecast, our web sites are already worth 80 per cent of our total asset value. Therefore, I've decided to delegate e-commerce management to our under-25s, who in turn have banished me to run the part of the company that makes a profit.

38

Better out than in

The other evening Alex looked up from her *Daily Mail* and stumped me with an ingenious enquiry. "Now they all have the euro," she said, "will Mars Bars cost the same in Paris as they do in Palermo?"

"I don't know," I replied.

"You studied economics and know all about business," Alex continued. "Tell me what difference the euro will make to us."

"It won't affect you," I said. "When we go to Portugal, you will produce your credit card as usual. But the euro would make a big difference to our business. £2m on new tills, 10,000 hours of staff training, and complaints from the consumer lobby if they think we have covered the extra cost by increasing prices. At least nothing will happen until Mr Brown decides whether we have passed his famous five tests."

"What are the famous tests?" said Alex, getting interested. I had to confess I hadn't a clue and decided to find out more in preparation for the possible referendum.

It took 30 minutes on the internet to find the five famous tests. There was no mention of them on the Treasury web site. I found them thanks to the *Daily Telegraph*.

Test one: How will the euro affect UK unemployment and prosperity?

I learned enough at university to know that economists are notoriously bad at predicting the future, but hopefully they know we are doing rather better than the rest of Europe and will follow the principle, "If it's not broken don't fix it."

Test two: What effect will the euro have on the UK financial services industry?

It seems unlikely that money lenders and exchange brokers in London will lose out, whatever happens to the euro. But some may be paranoid that Frankfurt will filch a bit of trade and put a dent in next year's bonus.

Test three: What effect will the euro have on investment in the UK?

The question is, will the Yanks and Japanese still put money our way if we are not in the euro-zone? Frankly, I doubt if it will make a halfpenny (or a cent) of difference. Some foreign investors may say they will pull out of a project because of the pound but, in reality, they invest in people not currencies. The euro won't alter the ability of the British workforce, but euro-zone working directives will push up the cost of employing them.

Test four: Is there sufficient flexibility in the UK economy to respond to shocks if we joined the euro-zone? Now I start to get nervous. This test recognises it won't be plain sailing. There is a clear indication that we could become members of a completely new club. It wouldn't be so bad if everyone became the same as us, but our friends in Europe expect us to become the same as them. Before we know it, they will not only have changed our money, but we will also be paying their higher rates of tax.

The final test: Is there sustainable convergence between the UK and the euro-zone economies? Put in plain English, are we moving in the same direction? Do we go up when they go up and do we go down when they go down? Convergence is the main issue that Gordon Brown has to examine. In doing so, he is acting like an index-tracker. This test has a hint of safety-first. No-one can blame the government as long as we are in step with our neighbours. Everything is all right as long as we are doing as well or as badly as everyone else in Europe. This is a trendy one-size-fits-all solution. But if one size does fit all, we must all buy the same product and with the euro that includes the Central European Bank and the European government. My business will receive a deluge of European directives and a paper mountain of euro forms so I can pay the higher levels of euro tax to subsidise the Mars bars in Palermo.

There is more to this euro than meets the eye, especially if you value your independence. I have been the subsidiary of a big plc and now thankfully have a private company with no other shareholders. I recognise the value of independence and the power of delegation. I call the way we operate "upside-down management." I want the staff in our shops to run the business, not to be euro-servants. I don't mind our national football team being run by a Swede, but I draw the line when our economy and, as a result, my business has rules set by the French and the Germans.

Now we hear Tony Blair is inclined towards the euro. He must have considered the political implications. Perhaps he wants to play on a bigger stage, or possibly he is frightened of failure. I wish our leader had the courage to go it alone and back Britain. I don't want to be another inflexible member of the European state. I much prefer to stay outside, avoid the safety of index-tracking and use our expertise to beat the market.

"I am glad you raised the subject of the euro," I said to Alex that night. "It has given me a real chance to think it through. I will certainly vote 'no' if a referendum comes."

"That's good," she said. "But you never said whether Mars Bars will be the same price in Paris as Palermo."

39

Going For Gold

One night, seven years ago I was falling asleep when I heard Alex, my wife, say "Sidney." "Sidney who?" I grunted. "Not Sidney..... Sydney. Now we can't see the games in Manchester, let's go to Australia." "Fine," I replied, turned over and forgot about it. But when Alex makes up her mind, it stays made up.

On Monday, 11th September, the day before departure, a steady stream of executives entered my office thinking my brain was already half way to Australia. They sensed I was a soft touch.

"Sorry to trouble you, I know you're very busy." simpered our office manager almost certainly wanting to spend more money. "I have completed a study of our telephone system. It desperately needs upgrading."

I don't know why he bothered. He knows I hate voice mail and I think it is wonderful that Doris answers on our switchboard with a cheerful, "hello how can I help?"

But I hadn't the stomach for an argument. "Let's talk about it after the Olympics".

Martin, my finance director wore his worried look. "The petrol crisis could knock sales sideways, I think we should put our shop development programme on hold until you get back."

Peter, our training manager, was even more cautious. "I am worried that your new Customer Care Campaign will be a flop. I cannot see it getting the support of the troops. Let's test it in ten shops to see if there is any enthusiasm."

Having had seeds of doubt subtly sown in my mind over all my pet projects, I was only too happy to go away.

It's easy to forget work when you are in Sydney. After two days sightseeing we had fallen in love with the city. Circular Quay, the Opera House, Darling Harbour, Sydney Harbour Bridge all dressed up for the Olympics. The place was buzzing.

We took a boat to Watsons Bay, had a sea food lunch at Doyles and returned through a fleet of Olympic yachtsmen practicing in Sydney Harbour, their coloured sails darting about like groups of tropical fish on the surface. It was magical.

This was the start of an enormous party. We could see why Sydney had won the vote over Manchester, it was simply no contest.

But the people were even more amazing than the city. On the bus into town strangers actually talked to each other, and young men stood up to let older women sit down. In Martin Place we were looking lost when a man asked us where we were heading and then took us half way there. I felt the whole population of Sydney had attended a customer care course, and indeed a lot of them had.

47,000 volunteers gave up six weeks of their time to wear the official uniform and help make the Sydney Olympic dream come true.

We set off to the Opening Ceremony two hours early, terrified of being trapped by traffic. We just missed our 2A bus, but another came four minutes later. The volunteer driver had been on the course. "Jump in and enjoy yourself, everybody on my bus wears a smile." We were in the stadium with an hour to spare.

I have not been on so many buses since I went to primary school. They took us and our Union Jacks to swimming, weightlifting, diving, hockey, equestrian cross country, basket ball, hand ball, rowing, sailing, gymnastics, volley ball, trampolining, baseball and several days of athletics.

We waved our flags for British gold in the rowing eights and for Jonathan Edwards in the long jump. We saw champion performances from Maurice Green, Michael Johnson, Venus Williams, Cathy Freeman and many more.

By day fourteen I was suffering from fatigue but the volunteers were still smiling. "How are you enjoying Sydney?" a smart grey bearded volunteer asked me. "It's great" I replied "but can I ask you a question?" "No worries," he smiled. "How did you find so many enthusiastic volunteers?"

"Oh that's easy, we love this city. It is a privilege to be part of the Olympic family." I walked off wondering how many volunteers we could have found to support the Millennium Dome.

On our final day we took a last look at Sydney Harbour. As I watched the ferry boat pulling out of Woolwich Pier, I posed the question everyone would ask when I got back home. "What was your most memorable moment?"

I saw some sensational scenes of success including the fabulous finish to the men's 1500 metres but I also witnessed the biggest failure of the Games and I will not forget it – it happened in the men's 4 x 200 metres freestyle swimming relay.

Kazakhstan's lead swimmer, Andrey Pakin, lent over the starting block to feel the temperature of the water, lost his balance and fell in. His team was disqualified for a false start.

What on earth did poor Andrey say to his three crestfallen team mates? One stamped out of the stadium and who can blame him. Two years training with six months on a special diet and four weeks in a training camp with no alcohol and no sex, and when you get to the Olympics, you are disqualified before you can take off your track suit.

I felt sorry for them but I felt especially sorry for Andrey. What was he going to tell his mother when he rang home? "Didn't make the final mum, I'll be home sooner than expected." I hope Andrey had the sense to buy his team mates the beers that night.

The home fans enjoyed too much success to note such glorious failure. Their constant cries of "Aussie Aussie Aussie, oi, oi,oi," worked well winning 16 gold medals. Their television covered every Australian performance in detail but paid little attention to the other competitors. I had to ring England to find out whether Denise Lewis had won the Heptathlon. But I don't want to appear a whingeing Pom – the Aussies deserve their sporting success. Nineteen million people who are sports mad. Wherever you go there are playing fields and posters advertising junior coaching.

My lasting memory of Sydney 2000 is not the stadium but our last journey on a 2A. The volunteer driver picked us up even though we were four hundred yards from his bus stop. I expressed my thanks as I climbed the step. "No worries," he said. "I hope you are enjoying Sydney because everyone on my bus wears a smile."

Forty-eight hours later I was back in the office. "Hi Peter." Our training manager was already hovering at my door. "Good trip?" "Great thanks. It was even better than I expected." "Had a good rest then?" "Yes, I did but…"

"Not been looking at shoe repairing shops, I hope."

"No, but I still learned an awful lot about the business."

40

Key Competencies

I was driving to the office following a game of real tennis, listening to Prime Minister's Question Time, when Tony Blair was asked about unemployment. "Thousands of businesses now benefit from 'New Deal'" he blustered. "Under this government everyone wins – workers, employees and the taxpayer." It made me think, because we are not a 'New Deal' winner. I rang Peter, our training manager, and asked him to meet me in the office.

Peter winced when I mentioned 'New Deal.' "Do you want the full story?" he asked, hoping I hadn't time to listen. "Go ahead," I said. "Tell me all about it."

"Can I start with NVQs?" asked Peter. "If you insist," I replied.

In 1990 I had attended several NVQ meetings with groups of drearily dressed *Guardian* readers from a training centre in Sheffield, three hard pressed independent cobblers and others who travelled a long way, said very little and completed an expense form on the way home. These terribly tedious meetings eventually bored me into resignation.

"Yes," said Peter, "I took your place on the Committee. Three years and 20 meetings later, SRITO (Shoe Repair Industry Training Organisation) launched the NVQ for shoe repairs. Sadly, SRITO was seriously under funded, so finding you in a fit of altruism, I persuaded you to acquire SRITO and give me responsibility for shoe repair NVQs. I am proud that in 18 months we helped 70 people gain the new qualification."

"Well done Peter, but you don't run SRITO now, did you lose interest?" I asked. "They changed the rules," he replied. "ITOs were replaced by National Training Organisations, which were larger and more efficient. We had to join with other trades. We objected strongly, sent out 18 copies of a 300 page report and complained to our local MP. It made no difference, cobblers were classed with tanners and shoe makers, people who didn't understand shoe repairs and key cutting. It's getting worse. NTOs could become ever bigger and we could be joined by textile workers, saddlers and veterinary surgeons. Our training advisors won't know a heel from a horse's hoof."

"So, you lost interest in NVQs," I persisted. "It's fairer to say NVQs lost interest in us. Our industry was too small to fit their master plan, NVQs might be good for some sectors, but didn't work for us. Mind you," continued Peter, puffing out his chest, "it gave time to concentrate on our own scheme which, I modestly suggest, has been a great success. 87 per cent of employees say our training is good or very good."

"Well done again, Peter, but what has this to do with 'New Deal?' Why aren't we one of Blair's winners?"

"Simple," said Peter, "they wouldn't let us join. Every 'New Deal' employee has to take an NVQ. We preferred our own training which does everything NVQs do and a lot more. The 'New Deal' unit studied our scheme for 18 months, but still said no."

"Why couldn't they extend NVQs to everything we do?" I asked. "That needed a new joint funded project," Peter explained. "You mean they wanted our money." I added. "No, not money," corrected Peter. "Our time and expenses. Anything connected with the project, in particular travelling, would count as our contribution to the new module." "So," I said, "The more we spend on our expenses, the more they like it. Perhaps that's why so many training managers travel first class." Peter looked perplexed. "But businesses only cover 51 per cent of the project cost."

"So," I asked, "who pays the other 49 per cent?"

"The government," said Peter. "They spend it on consultants." I started to understand. "You mean the more time and money we spend, the more government can pay these consultants."

"That's right." said Peter. "Would it be cynical," I suggested, "to say the consultants get paid because we spend time and money travelling to tell them all about our business, so they can tell the civil servants, who then tell us what to do?"

"Got it." said Peter. "That's why I thought it better to use our own training scheme and forget about NVQs. I am sorry, in the process, you failed to be a 'New Deal' winner."

I clearly didn't look convinced. Not happy?" asked Peter. "I'll give you some homework." He produced a pile of NVQ paperwork which ruined my next weekend.

I started with the 1997 report on Occupational Mapping in the Shoe Repair Industry, which concluded: "We should proceed to review and develop relevant NVQs to cater for shoe repairing, key cutting and engraving. The award should be constructed with a common mandatory core and function specific optional units."

By Monday morning I was familiar with NVQ terminology. Key competences, unit overview, performance objectives, knowledge requirements. "A lot of it is gobbledegook," I told Peter when we next met. "You don't understand," said Peter. "All NVQs are like that. It's their standard format." I was bemused. "You mean there is a special way that NVQs are written?"

"Yes that's right," said Peter. "Do I detect scope for an NVQ for people who write "NVQs?" I asked. "For goodness sake don't tell them that," said Peter, "or they will call in another consultant!"

I was beginning to think we were Luddites out on a limb knocking a New Labour success. My faith was restored at a dinner the following night for companies listed by the *Sunday Times* as 'Great Places to Work.' I quizzed a big retailer who was high on the list. "How many of your people are involved in NVQ?" I asked. "None," she replied. "We concentrate on in-house training. Our employees like it."

At least we can still opt out of government schemes and go our own way, but soon we may have to obey Brussels, and before long our business could be a load of Euro Cobblers.

When I next saw Peter, I apologised. "I now understand why we weren't a 'New Deal' winner. Incidentally, how much did the footwear repair NVQ cost?" "Good question," said Peter. "If you include money spent by the industry, consultants and, of course, the Training Agency, you will be close to £2m." "Final question, Peter. How many shoe repairers are currently following an NVQ? Peter smiled as he replied. "Two."

Outside the office

That grand old politician Denis Healey rightly observed that everybody should have a hinterland – the interests, passions and concerns that round out what might be an otherwise two-dimensional professional life. John's hinterland is as diverse as it is wide, ranging from the conventional (the perennial battles with the golf course) to the extraordinary short-term fostering of some 80 children.

41

Stop the clocks

For some time, I have watched well-known high-street names disappear before my very eyes. Some years ago, we lost MacFisheries, Timothy Whites and John Collier. More recently, we have seen the end of Saxone, Freeman Hardy & Willis – and are soon to witness the closure of Richard Shops. Now the papers are telling us that British Homes Stores and Laura Ashley are struggling; not to mention the problems at Marks & Spencer.

Troubled retail companies blame high stocks and big markdowns for their decreasing profits. And, of course, there's the weather. But what can you expect if you live in the UK? The weather is something we all complain about. It is completely unreasonable to expect snow in the winter and sunshine in the summer. This is where my idea comes to the rescue.

Like all the best ideas, my proposal is extremely simple. All we do is move the year by six weeks, leaving the weather where it is. That means we get July's weather in the middle of May and mid-February's weather at Christmas.

But how will this help fashion retailers? Let me take you through their trading year, starting in the spring. At the beginning of March, summer clothes appear in the shop windows and the poor retailers sit around through April and well into May waiting for the warm weather. By the time the "heatwave" arrives in July, they have already cut their prices and started the sale.

Under my system, that July heatwave will arrive in the middle of May – just right for the peak selling season. Sales will increase; stock levels will fall. The July sale will be launched while we are enjoying the sunshine that nowadays almost always occurs towards the end of August.

Take the autumn/winter season. The way things are now, autumn stock arrives in the middle of an Indian summer. Boots and heavy coats are available for sale while the potential customers are sunbathing in September. There is nothing like snow and ice to shift winter stock. In the UK, it doesn't often snow until the end of January – well after all the boots and coats have been reduced for the winter sale.

Here again my system comes to the rescue. Snow and ice will arrive before Christmas, and there is even a chance of a cold snap in October.

So that's my great idea – to move the year by six weeks, to boost sales, reduce markdowns and increase profits. The high street will be a much happier place.

I imagine you are already searching out the snag – apart from the obvious one of trying to persuade Brussels to make the move. The real difficulty is finding a way of changing the calendar without causing any great disruption.

Somehow we have to make sure the year doesn't stand still for six weeks. We must stick on exactly the same date for 42 days.

I did think that March 24 would be a good day to do this, particularly as it is my birthday. I would receive birthday presents for 42 days running. But in the process will rapidly reach the age of 98!

A much better idea is to stop the year on December 25, so that every day can be Christmas Day for six whole weeks. But the shops don't open on Christmas Day, so the very businesses I am trying to save would have six weeks of taking no money at all. Even worse, December 25 is a quarter-day – one of the four days of the year when we pay rent to the landlord. It's not something retailers want to do for 42 days running.

If the year stopped on Christmas Day, my great plan would probably have killed off every retailer in the land before it works in their favour.

I thought I would have to cast my idea on the scrap heap until I realised what a disaster the millennium is going to be. I am not talking about the millennium bug; I'm talking about the millennium hangover.

The government has already declared an extra bank holiday to help everyone recover from the festivities. I have no doubt that the public will turn that one bank holiday into another full week off. But don't think they are going to spend the time shopping. The high street will probably be deserted for the whole of January.

So the solution is obvious. Let's just stop on December 31, 1999 for six weeks. It will give us another 42 days to cure the millennium bug, so that everyone can have a party they'll never forget. And once we've all recovered, we'll have a high street that makes money. And Marks & Spencer will be saved from further embarrassment.

42

Mustique man

I don't intend to retire. I plan to add an extra day's holiday every year. This year I need to be away nine weeks, so I started in January by going to Mustique.

I arrived home on February 6 to find a letter from *Real Business*. "Dear John, change of plan, we now need something for April, can we have your column by end-Feb?"

Stuck for a topic, I sought advice. "As you've hardly seen the office for six weeks, why not write about holidays?" said my wife Alex.

I have had a lot of time off recently, but I don't count Christmas as a holiday. When I started work in 1960, Christmas lasted two days.

Last year the world stopped on December 23 and stayed asleep until January 3.

I did my best to conform. It started well – a carol service on Christmas Eve, turkey on Christmas Day and a Boxing Day win for Manchester City all achieved without a glance into my briefcase. On December 28, I started sorting out photographs that had been in a drawer for the past three years.

On December 29, I abandoned the photographs and went to the office. It was wonderful. It was so peaceful and productive that I went back the following day. The secret must have got out; I found ten others at their desks mixing their "did you have a nice one?" with "it's great to be back to normal."

But we couldn't get back to normal; we had to face the millennium and the flu. I greeted the New Year with a nasty virus but recovered by January 3 and went to work.

I made a New Year's Resolution to be pleasant to Barbara, my long-suffering secretary. It wasn't difficult. She returned to work with a spring in her step; my holiday was only three weeks away.

Barbara is always efficient but is at her very best when I am about to go away. The desk was cleared, loose ends tied up. Two days before departure, passports, driving licence, tickets and travellers cheques were all neatly presented. She even kept smiling when I checked the documents to see if she had made a mistake.

I set Saturday aside for packing, but returned from the golf course to find Alex had already selected my clothes, leaving me to write the luggage labels and pick something to read.

After I had rechecked the money, tickets and passports, I packed four books I had been given for Christmas together with The Crisis of Global Capitalism by George Soros (which has now been abroad four times and still not been read beyond page five).

Shortly after we got married, Alex taught me how to mix business with holidays. You don't. Family trips to Cornwall and Portugal left no time for work. I experienced what is now known as "quality time" with our children, an assault course that showed Alex's day job to be considerably more demanding than mine.

Despite this frantic family bonding, my mind still wandered towards work. I telephoned the office every day and they sent me figures once a week. I worried about all the problems but had no time to think of any solutions.

Nowadays I don't ring the office. But if we go away without the children, I'm allowed to take a little work instead. It's just the time to tackle a pet project that has slipped down the action list. I have written a training manual on the Isle of Lewis and devised a customer care programme in St Lucia.

The outline for the book we are shortly to publish was written in Mustique. So it seemed reasonable to take the final draft back to the island for editing – "should be finished in four days," I told Alex. After three days, I had only done a fifth of the job. Alex was very good about it. "Just guarantee one thing," she said. "When you have finished, that will be it, no more writing." I promised. "No problem," I said. "They don't even need an article for the April magazine, they're using an extract from the book instead."

I finished editing the book on the last day of our holiday and drank a Mustique Whammy at Basil's Bar to celebrate.

As soon as I got home, I raced to the study to see what had happened while I was away. I found the usual bills, junk mail and reasons why there had been little progress after a recent board meeting. Buried at the bottom of the memos was the letter saying that *Real Business* wouldn't feature the book until May.

I met their deadline. This article was delivered on February 29, a week before I went away again. In exchange, I received the final proof of my book for checking.

Postcard from Antigua, March 10. Just arrived – plan to read lots of books but have put final proof in the suitcase. The holiday gives me a good chance to check it without interruption. Feel sure Alex will understand.

43

Father's pride

This month's column isn't the usual light-hearted Timpo romp through the executive corridors of power. This is your editor's fault. He asked me to write about the work that my wife Alex and I do as foster carers.

Alex was never cut out for committees or meeting ladies who lunch. When asked to put her main occupation on a form, she writes "mother." So when our third child reached school age, she looked for new ways to use her qualifications as a nanny. She saw an advert in the local paper. Cheshire social services were looking for foster parents. She applied, we passed the test and, 73 foster children later, Alex still comes back for more.

We were naïve when we started. We'd had three children – we thought we knew everything about child care. It was common sense: three meals a day, regular bedtimes and some tender loving care were all that was needed.

We were in for a shock. The first two boys, aged four and three, came with cigarette burns on their feet and rather colourful language. For the first week they spent hours riding a small push-bike around our kitchen shouting, "f*** off, f*** off."

During the next six months we introduced them to bedtime stories, walks in the park, trips to the seaside, "please" and "thank you." The boys learned a lot but Alex still had her own tough lessons to learn.

Our first foster children left a fortnight before Christmas and went to a local children's home. (Twenty years ago, short-term foster care meant a maximum of six months; today, the children stay until a permanent home is found.) Alex was heartbroken, making regular visits to peer through a fence to see if the two boys were in the playground.

It was a hard lesson, but Alex learned to avoid intense emotional involvement with the stream of children who have since appeared in our home.

We usually get a few days' warning, but some children arrive within an hour of the first call. That's part of the buzz. Suddenly, life takes on a different tempo. Alex reorganises bedrooms and I trot off with a shopping list that may include baby food and nappy liners.

Shopping with foster children can be interesting. On my first day as a foster carer, I took the two boys to a posh bakers. The elder boy tugged my arm shouting, "look John, that woman has got big busters."

Some children came to us because mum was in hospital or prison, or simply couldn't cope. Many others came from a life of abuse.

Two children had a particularly tough time. The girl had burns up both her legs; she had been held against a gas fire. Her brother had severe bruising on his head, having been bashed against the wall. Both brother and sister had festering wounds across their backs, caused by a fishing rod. All this left emotional damage. The girl played bizzare games with our daughter's dolls house. She turned all the furniture upside-down. "Dad's got a nowt on," she said. Her brother relieved his anger on our garden frames, taking a hammer to 60 panes of glass.

Some children never fully adjust. Our adopted son, Oliver, who came to us when he was six, still has problems at the age of 24. His various attempts to work for our business have always ended in tears.

Each child brings a new challenge. I was a guest speaker in London one night last year when, after the formal speeches were over, I turned to the chairman. "Do you mind if I make a telephone call, my wife is expecting a baby."

The baby had arrived during my speech, after spending six months in hospital where she was born addicted to heroin (her mother was a heroin addict). The baby screamed all night for weeks but gradually recovered enough for us to believe she will lead a normal life.

Some of the most damaging abuse is mental rather than physical. A four-year-old child was very aggressive when he first came. If we told him off, he responded with, "shut it you f***ing bastard." Then he would lie on the floor screaming with rage. He had every reason to be angry. When a social worker asked his mother what he was like, she replied, "he's just a little shit."

I did warn you this was not my normal light-hearted look at life, but child abuse is serious. One in four children is being subjected to abuse right now and, as a result, more behaviour problems are being stored up for the next 20 years.

So in the spirit of Christmas, what can be done? I am not suggesting that you should change your lives by becoming a foster carer, but if you do think it a good idea, the first step is to contact your local social services department. You will find their number in the phone book. An easier way to help is by supporting the NSPCC which is running a major campaign right now.

44

Giving my money away

When I walked into the office one day last month, my secretary Barbara was getting testy with someone on the phone. "Mr Timpson is in a meeting, can I ask what you are ringing about?" As she listened to the reply, she made a face. "There is no need to be rude," she said firmly and stuck out her tongue. "Would you believe it, he hung up."

I did believe it. People can be pretty rude on the phone. "He wouldn't say what it was about," huffed Barbara. "Probably another charity, some people think we are a soft touch." This month's appeals include the Common Cold Research Centre, Oswestry Opera House, the Miles Platting Monument and the Donkey Sanctuary. "I always say that our charity budget is already committed, but they don't listen," Barbara observed. "Oh, and I nearly forgot, that nice editor at *Real Business* rang. Can you call him back?"

My editor answered after two rings. "You have a reputation for care in the community," he announced. "So that's why we get those begging phone calls," I muttered, but he didn't hear. "Did you read the June magazine?" he asked. "Yes, and that cartoon makes me look fatter in every issue. My children say I have put on five stone in six months..." "I wasn't talking about your article," he said, ignoring my criticism, "but the piece about companies with a social mission. Our readers want to hear more. Can you say how generosity helps your business?"

Charity was a problem for our business until the NSPCC invited me to a dinner. I knew I would eventually have to pay up for accepting the free meal, but my wife Alex liked the idea of dinner with the Duke of Westminster. "All you will have to do is put a few pounds in the raffle," she said.

But there wasn't a raffle and I never touched my wallet all evening. On the way home Alex was enthused. "That was a great evening. You must do something special to thank them." I saw an opportunity, the solution to my charity problem. "I will make the NSPCC our charity of the year, then I can refuse anyone else who asks for money." "That's fine," said Alex, "but still do your bit for the NSPCC."

I was awake until 3am worrying about what to do. I told Alex my solution as I poured the early-morning tea. "Bits of glue and lots of holes," I said. "What on earth are you talking about?" said Alex wearily. "Well, we do lots of jobs for free, like glueing soles and putting holes in belts. If we ask those customers to give to the NSPCC, it should bring in £500 a week. We could make a video to encourage employees to support the fund-raising. We could organise sponsored walks, run in the London Marathon..." "You're all talk," interrupted Alex. "It will be forgotten before you even get into the office. All you think about is shoes, keys and bloody watch repairs."

Eight weeks later we showed the video to our area managers and collected £200 within ten minutes. With some trepidation I sent the video in plain brown Jiffy bags to every employee's home. Some were suspicious, but I shouldn't have worried about how streetwise shoe repairers would respond to a charity appeal. In the first week our shops collected £3,000. Within a month they were running their own fund-raising events. Alan in Stafford sat outside his shop on a Saturday, had all his hair shaved off – and collected £400. Bob in Taunton had his chest waxed and raised £3,000 (£1 per hair!). Over 20 months we raised £240,000. And it wasn't just the NSPCC treasurer who was happy. Customers appreciated their free job more because the donation gave it value. Alex was happy that we had followed her ideas, and I enjoyed record profits. Most of all, our staff were proud of being part of a company with a conscience.

Fund-raising has now become an important part of Timpson life. This year each region was asked to choose its own charity. Merseyside selected Cystic Fibrosis and the Potteries picked their local hospice. The rest support ChildLine and are raising £2,000 a week.

We also contribute to lots of other causes dear to employees' hearts. Our newsletter features "Captain Cash" (alias my son James) who gives up to £250 to good causes every week. Over the last few months Captain Cash has bought a football team strip, funded a special-needs teacher at a local school and helped send a manager's daughter to have medical treatment abroad.

I could say much more about the hidden benefits of a social conscience but my editor only gives me one page. If you don't have a company charity, I suggest you get one. If you are stuck for a cause, choose ChildLine, founded by Esther Rantzen. It is the only Samaritan service for kids. Its £8m total funds only support enough volunteers to answer one-third of the children who ring up. You will be helping a good cause and whenever you receive begging phone calls you can reply, "We already have our charity of the year." Adopting a national charity has been a great advantage. Barbara says she wouldn't be without one.

Epilogue

45

Risk Assessment

I was clearing my desk before going on holiday, when this book's editor Stuart Rock rang. "Got an idea for the last chapter," he said. "Why don't you write a summary saying how you see the business today."

Alex says holidays and work don't mix but I had no choice. Stuart only gave me three weeks for the task. How could I write when Alex wasn't looking? We had taken five teenagers and a nine-year-old for a week in the Algarve. Go karts, water park, tennis, driving range, beach bar, banana ride, it was non-stop action with children in your face all the time except when the 15 year olds went to the night club. They drank and I was expected to drive. My job was to pick them up at 3 o'clock every morning. "Don't complain," said Alex "you can have a lie in." So I wrote this piece in the middle of the night.

The articles in this book portray me as a whinger, complaining about employment regulations, e-mails, accountants, voice mail, meetings and mobile 'phones. But far from whinging about business, the last 43 years have been full of positive experiences.

Things were a lot different when I started. We could advertise for counter girls at £3.17s.9d a week, while I was paid the boy's rate of £5.7s.6d. Sixty-five per cent of shoes in the shops were made in the UK, we didn't use computers, there were no traffic jams − so we simply complained about the weather, especially the smog.

A lot has changed, but business fundamentals remain the same. With a degree in industrial economics from Nottingham University and the precocious confidence of youth, I set out with a completely false idea of what makes a business tick. I thought it was like playing Monopoly, making decisions and telling everyone what to do. I believed success was created by market research and a business plan −

the right pricing policy wrapped in a proper marketing campaign. If the plan led to budgets that everyone had to follow, all would be well. If things went wrong, you fired a few managers and devised a draconian round of cost cutting. Eventually I discovered the realities of management. During 43 years, the knowledge gained at Nottingham University has been modified by the University of Life.

My first job in a Clarks children's shoe factory was simple. I just had to buckle up sandals. To earn a bonus, I needed to do more than 120 pairs an hour. Everyone else did it easily but in three months I never earned a penny bonus. It taught me to respect the skill of people in the front line.

I believed business could be run by a set of rules. Following a terrible season for women's fashion shoes, I carried out a detailed examination of past sales to produce some rules for the buying department. Don't buy coloured shoes, avoid heels over three inches, two-tone shoes and high-leg boots - and never buy white sandals. Fashion moves in a cycle – in two years my rules became a recipe for disaster. Good entrepreneurs don't just use past facts to forecast the future.

In the seventies shoe retailing was dominated by the British Shoe Corporation. They were the biggest and the best but they were arrogant, bullied suppliers and paid lip service to their customers. Every shop had a customer complaint limit of two per cent, but their shoes fell to bits at the rate of four per cent, so half the justified complaints were rejected. Eventually, customers stopped coming back to British Shoe and their 25 per cent market share dwindled to seven per cent before they finally disappeared. Even the biggest businesses have to look after their customers.

At Nottingham University I heard about the Hawthorn experiment, where psychologists increased the lighting in a factory and production improved, then they reduced the lighting to the previous level and production rose further.

I never believed it until we changed our key cutting display. Every three years we alter the colour of our key board and, as a result, sales always go up. It provides our people with an excuse for doing better, and nearly every change that is welcomed by our shop staff increases sales. We should never stand still.

I visit as many shops as I can every year, I owe this obsession to the examples set by my father and my grandfather. Inititially, I wasn't too sure why they did it, I know now, it's the best way to find out what is going on.

There is another way to get the facts. Gather together a group of six to ten of your people and get them talking; they soon tell you what you need to know. Personal contact is much better than market research.

Two years ago I spent a day with Lee Nicholls – our area manager in London – on the day of a Tube strike. We met at our shop near Victoria Station at 8.00am. He had already reorganised the staff rota and every shop was open. No mean feat when many couldn't get to the shop where they normally work. I could never do what Lee did that day. Thankfully, the chairman doesn't need the skills of an area manager.

I learned an important lesson from our biggest competitor, Mr Minit. In 1996, the Swiss bank UBS acquired the Minit business. I was interested in buying their poorly-performing British operation, so I arranged to meet the British executive behind the deal. I got a frosty reception. He said they were experts at putting professional management into family businesses – once they had worked their miracle on Minit, they would be ready to transform Timpson. It was a short meeting and I was soon sitting at a café outside the UBS office. I now had a serious competitor with unlimited finance and the muscle to wipe me off the High Street, what was I going to do? I decided the only way to compete was to become the best at what we do, the best at shoe repairs, key cutting and engraving and to offer customers the best possible service. We had to have the best people who were so loyal they would not join the opposition. We needed to look after our people both through pay and pastoral care.

Within 15 minutes I produced the formula we have followed for seven years. Training is ingrained in our culture. We now spend five per cent of our turnover on training, including manuals written in pictures rather than words and customer care courses for all.

We hunted for ways to look after our people better. We introduced a hardship fund, holiday homes, a social programme and regular weekly newsletters. We discovered how to give customers excellent service. It's simple, trust staff to do it for you, you can't give good service by a set of rules. To provide a truly personal service, shop staff must have total authority to do what they think is best for every customer.

We also discovered the principle of trust also applies to middle management. In 1999 we had a period when sales dropped and costs were rising. The result was a big drop in profit. We thought about a major cost cutting campaign but instead introduced a bonus scheme for area managers, our key field executives. They got ten per cent of any profit improvement and quickly saw that 10p in each pound of cost savings went on their salary. We will never launch another cost cutting scheme from head office, now we trust our middle managers to do the job.

The Timpson business philosophy is totally based on trust. We trust our people to run the business and are there to help when they have a problem. We call it "upside-down management."

It has taken me 43 years to discover the power of trust. This principle is now being followed by James, but he won't find it easy. I am wary of the future – he is bound to face some shocks and surprises. The warning sign was clearly written on the swimming pool at our villa in Portugal. It was a magnificent pool with a wonderful diving board, but at the eight-foot-deep end, a notice said, 'no diving.' It was the owner's way of avoiding blame and any claim for compensation.

We live in a world of paranoid professionals who profit from insecurity and disloyalty. They advise management to mistrust everyone and are amazed to find we trust our employees, our customers and our suppliers. I suppose we run a risk. Some people think we are foolhardy, a soft touch and unprofessional, but I remember from Nottingham that one of the definitions of profit is the reward for taking risks. Over the next few years James will be governed by more laws and regulations based on lack of trust drawn up by prophets of doom. We are already paying for the ambulance chasing blame society, with the rising costs of insurance and pensions. Strict employment law will stop us paying people the best wages and the Trade Descriptions Act could prevent us being proper entrepreneurs on the High Street.

Despite all this regulation, people still talk fondly of empowerment and delegation, so my "upside-down management" should be flavour of the month. But it is very different from the way most people view delegation. Institutions are happy to delegate responsibility but keep authority. "Upside-down management" works the other way round. We delegate authority but still keep the responsibility. Think about it.

Institutional delegation results in targets, like the waiting lists that hospitals manipulate and A-level results. Recently I had first hand experience of a government target. Following a fraudulent transaction on my credit card, I contacted our local police station. The substantial sum involved should have commanded considerable attention from the constable on the 'phone. "You are through to the wrong station," he told me. "You don't live in Wythenshawe, ring Cheshire." I rang Cheshire. "The crime was committed in London," they said. "It's not our patch." I spoke to Chelsea who claimed it could be the responsibility of a station in the West End. Although there was CCTV evidence and the culprit's address I heard nothing for two weeks. I rang Cheshire Police and asked why. "To be honest," said the constable, "we are not targeted for this job, so there is no need to hurry."

Over the next 20 years there will be more restrictions rather than less. Our government – whatever its politics – will tie us up with more red tape. Plenty more directives will come from Europe. Every change – whether it is health and safety, employment law or pensions – will have to be paid for. Not only will we incur extra costs in the business, but taxes will increase to fund the civil servants that check we have carried out each new directive. We can only hope that one day governments will realise that we are over-managed and over-regulated. In the meantime, I will continue to work on the principle that profit is the reward for taking risks and the best way to run a business is to trust people. All the evidence I have seen shows that trust is a risk worth taking.